R · PLAN ·
= 1:0"
VATION

30'-0"   25'-4"

28'-6¼"

1'-5"

30'-0"   46'-6½"

34'-0"

28'

·SCALE· FOR· PLAN· ᲚELEVATION·

10 14 18 112 116 120 124 128 132 136 140 144 148 152 156 160 164 FEET

D1608360

NOTE:
FOLLOWING · ISSUE · OF ·
THE · MONOGRAPH · SERIES ·
WILL · CONTAIN · MEASURED ·
DRAWINGS · OF · THE · INTERIOR ·
OF · THE · BRICE · HOUSE ·

MEAS ᲢDRAWN · KENNETH · CLARK·

E V A T I O N ·   · S E C T I O N ·

E · H O U S E ·

M A R Y L A N D ·

NA730 .M4 G46 1988

The Georgian heritage

THE GEORGIAN HERITAGE

Other National Historical Society Publications:

THE IMAGE OF WAR: 1861–1865

TOUCHED BY FIRE: A PHOTOGRAPHIC PORTRAIT OF THE CIVIL WAR

WAR OF THE REBELLION: OFFICIAL RECORDS
   OF THE UNION AND CONFEDERATE ARMIES

OFFICIAL RECORDS OF THE UNION AND CONFEDERATE NAVIES
   IN THE WAR OF THE REBELLION

HISTORICAL TIMES ILLUSTRATED ENCYCLOPEDIA OF THE CIVIL WAR

A TRAVELLER'S GUIDE TO GREAT BRITAIN SERIES

For information about National Historical Society Publications, write:
Historical Times, Inc., 2245 Kohn Road, Box 8200, Harrisburg, Pennsylvania 17105

Architectural Treasures of Early America

THE GEORGIAN HERITAGE

From material originally published as
The Georgian Period
edited by
Professor William Rotch Ware

Lisa C. Mullins, Editor

Roy Underhill, Consultant

A Publication of
THE NATIONAL HISTORICAL SOCIETY

89-16

Copyright © 1988 by the National Historical Society

All rights reserved. Printed in the United States of America. No part of this book may be used or reproduced in any manner whatsoever without written permission except in the case of brief quotations emobodied in critical articles and reviews.

Library of Congress Cataloging-in-Publication Data

The Georgian heritage/Lisa C. Mullins, editor; Roy Underhill, consultant.
    (Architectural treasures of Early America; 15)
    1. Architecture, Georgian—Massachusetts. 2. Architecture, Colonial—Massachusetts. 3. Architecture—Massachusetts.
4. Architecture, Georgian—Massachusetts—Boston.
5. Architecture, Colonial—Massachusetts—Boston.
6. Architecture—Massachusetts—Boston. 7. Boston (Ma.)—
Buildings, structures, etc. 8. Architecture—England—
Influence. 9. Architecture—Ireland—Influence.
I. Mullins, Lisa C. II. Series. III. Series: Architectural treasures of Early America (Harrisburg, Pa.); 15.
NA730.M4G46 1988   720'.9744—dc19   88-1676
ISBN 0-918678-37-4

CONTENTS

SONG OF THE CARPENTER

"The house-carpenter has somehow lacked a poet to sing his praises. . . ." So says Paul Waterhouse in Chapter 1 of this volume. Yet, while the poets have not necessarily sung their praises, carpenters have figured in literature since Noah built the ark.

Carpenters were themselves responsible for some of the poetry of the late Middle Ages, as their guild presented mystery pageants for the townsfolk. In about 1500, some anonymous word-wright roughed out *The Debate of the Carpenter's Tools*. In it, the tools argue the virtue or futility of honest labor. Here, the broad axe used to smooth the timbers takes the optimistic stance:

> The broad axe seyd withouten miss,
> He seyd: the plane my brother is;
> We two schall clense and make full plain,
> That no man schall us geyne-seyne,
> And gete our mayster in a year
> More sylver than a man may bere.

The years after the Great Fire of London were good for the building trades. Joseph Moxon's 1678 *Mechanick Exercises, or the Doctrine of Handyworks* was among the earliest of the honored line of how-to books, revealing the secrets of the trades to anyone who could read. His was a sympathetic view:

> And tho' the Mechanicks be, by some, accounted
> Ignoble and Scandalous, yet it is very well known,
> that many Gentlemen in this Nation, of good Rank
> and high Quality, are conversant in Handy-Works . . .
> How pleasant and healthey this their Diversion is,

Simple acts such as snapping a chalk-line take on a lyric quality in Moxon's words. But Moxon did not shrink from the coarser amusements of his subject:

> A little trick is sometimes used among some (that would be thought cunning Carpenters) privately to touch the Head of the Nail with a little Ear-wax, and then lay a Wager with a Stranger to the Trick, that he shall not drive that Nail up to the Head with so many Blows. The Stranger thinks he shall assuredly win, but does assuredly lose; for the Hammer no sooner touches the Head of the Nail, but instead of entering the Wood it flies away, notwithstanding his utmost care in striking it down-right . . .

As the evils of industrialization spread through England, the village carpenter acquired a noble, nostalgic glow. In *Adam Bede,* English novelist George Eliot, whose own father was a carpenter, painted a joiner's shop "as it appeared on the eighteenth of June, in the year of our Lord 1799":

> The afternoon sun was warm on the five workmen there, busy upon doors and window-frames and wainscoting. A scent of pine-wood from a tent-like pile of

planks outside the open door mingled itself with the scent of the elder-bushes which were spreading their summer snow close to the open window opposite; the slanting sunbeams shone through the transparent shavings that flew before the steady plane, and lit up the fine grain of the oak panelling which stood propped against the wall.

The earliest American writers were more concerned with the rigors of survival than the beauty of labor. William Stith described the trials of the brave gentlemen of Jamestowne, Virginia, in 1608:

> . . . they soon made it their delight, to hear
> Trees thunder, as they fell; and afterwards became
> very hardy, useful, and resolute Men, . . . But the
> Axes often blistering their tender Fingers, they
> would, at every third Stroke, drown the Echo, with
> a loud Volley of Oaths.

After seven generations of adjustment, American hands were tougher. Benjamin Franklin noted in his 1771 *Autobiography* how quickly the men felled trees to build a fort during a wilderness expedition:

> Seeing the trees fall so fast, I had the
> curiosity to look at my watch when two men began to
> cut at a pine; in six minutes they had it upon the
> ground, and I found it of fourteen inches diameter.

In Walt Whitman's *Song of The Broad-Axe* the celebration of work neared its peak:

> The house-builder at work in cities or anywhere,
> The preparatory jointing, squaring, sawing, morticing,
> The hoist-up of beams, the push of them in their places,
>   laying them regular,
> Setting the studs by their tenons in the mortices
>   according as they were prepared,
> The blows of mallets and hammers, the attitudes of the
>   men, their curv'd limbs,
> Bending, standing, astride the beams, driving in pins,
>   holding on by posts and braces,

Whitman watched, but the song of experience is the greatest poetry. Near the end of March, 1845, Henry Thoreau "borrowed an axe and went down to the woods by Walden Pond." Although his cabin may seem far removed from the work of the Georgian carpenters, his appreciation is universal:

> Shall we forever resign the pleasure of construction to the carpenter? What does architecture amount to in the experience of the mass of men? I have never in all my walks came across a man engaged in so simple and natural an occupation as building his house.

ROY UNDERHILL
MASTER HOUSEWRIGHT
COLONIAL WILLIAMSBURG

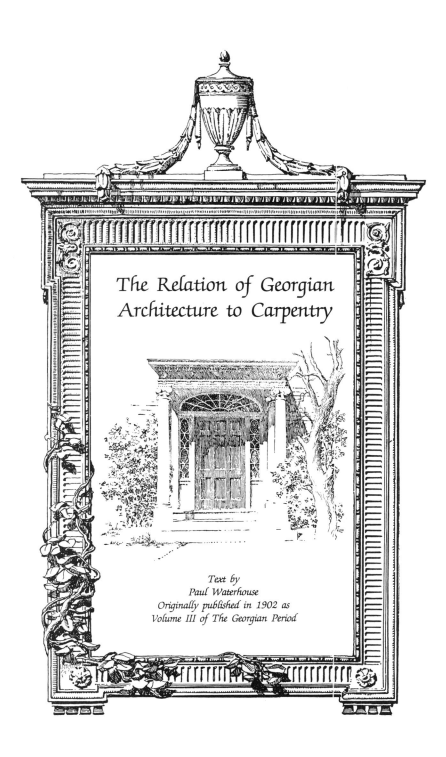

The Relation of Georgian Architecture to Carpentry

Text by
Paul Waterhouse
Originally published in 1902 as
Volume III of The Georgian Period

Fig. 1. GODFREY HOUSE, HOLLINGBOURNE, KENT
Built 1587, restored 1859.

THE RELATION OF GEORGIAN ARCHITECTURE TO CARPENTRY

SMALL need is there for any one to be at pains to prove the importance of timber-work as an element in English domestic architecture. The very paucity of our evidences of the earlier methods of British house-building is in itself a testimony to the prevalence of wood as the principal means of construction. The students of mediaeval architecture sometimes wonder why it is that the subjects offered for their consideration are nearly always churches, sometimes castles, and but seldom houses. And the main reason for this disproportionate survival of religious buildings is, no doubt, the simple fact that the Englishman of the Middle Ages, and indeed of later times, though he associated stone with his ideas of church-building, used timber of choice and of necessity for the walls of his own house. Fire and old age have made clearance of these wooden homes, but have left the masonry of the cathedrals. Even churches, as we know, were built of timber in the first days of British Christianity, and if we can realize the fact that the primitive English places of worship were not only very small, but of very light wooden construction, and perhaps without any foundations, we shall appreciate the possibility of there being more human force than miracle in the feat of St. Dunstan, who, with a thrust of his strong shoulder, corrected the orientation of a chancel which did not duly face the East.

It might almost be said that the history of English domestic architecture has been a record of the progressive rejection of timber. Today we are within easy distance of building houses in which there is no timber at all; we have certainly achieved the power of dispensing with wood as a constructive element, and, indeed, we exercise this power to such an extent that there are houses of which it could be claimed that they contain no wood except such as is there for decorative purposes — and for doors. Our floors, our very roofs, we make of concrete and steel, our stairs are stone or concrete, our windowframes are iron or gun-metal, and, though one may enter a room which appears to have a wooden chimney-piece and a painted deal dado, the chances are that you will find the former to be cast-iron and the latter some composition of asbestic plaster. The wooden door, it must be owned, dies hard, but I saw a door, apparently of mahogany, the other day which, its creator proudly declared, was mainly composed of a new species of fireproof papier-maché! Except on grounds of fire prevention, this successful contest against the work of the carpenter and joiner is a spectacle of the most melancholy kind — most melancholy and most modern. For, though the struggle has, in a sense, been going on through all the ages, the conclusion that wherever a substitute can be found for wood it should be used in preference to it is a product of entirely modern reasoning. Even in the days of the eighteenth century the verdict in the battle of materials was wont to go the other way. In fact, it might be stated as a general proposition that the architects of the Georgian period believed in their inmost hearts that in spite of the rivalry of other materials, there was really in the long run nothing like wood. The versatile Dean Aldrich, in his Latin treatise on the elements of architecture, bids his readers, if they would secure a sound foundation, lay the footings of their walls on trunks of trees; and those of us who are engaged in London architecture are aware that a frequent source of unexpected expense in street building is the necessity for cutting out of the old party-walls (under the peremptory orders of a district-surveyor) the "bond-timbers," without which our forefathers considered a

Fig. 2. WESLEY'S COTTAGE, ROLVENDEN LAYNE, KENT

brick structure incomplete. In fact, it would almost seem as if even a hundred years ago the builders of houses, while realizing the usefulness of brick and stone, were still scientifically convinced that, for real stability, unity and solidity in any fabric, timber was a necessity.

But we must go back for a while and look at the antecedents, in order that we may see what stages led up to that phase of English architecture which, when carried oversea and translated into Colonial terms, took so kindly to its new climate, and seemed to find in the luxuriant timber supply of the New World not so much a need for any modification of its methods as an opportunity for fuller realization and development on the original lines.

Timber construction had taken several forms in British architecture. The most familiar, perhaps the most typical, form of timber exterior is that which presents itself in Chester and the neighborhood, and which we know as "half-timbering." Its structural origin is very simple: it consists of the primal elements of wooden

formation. However wooden walls may be finished, they consist essentially of some form of framework which would not of itself exclude the weather, having interstices between its structural posts. The necessary continuous solidity of the walls is secured either by filling these interstices or by covering the whole formation. In the case of the half-timbering it is the former method which is adopted. The posts, which are the elements of the fabric, are exposed and the intermediate spaces are filled-in with plastering. The richer and more elaborate examples of this much admired, but sometimes *bizarre,* style of art are well known, and are fully illustrated in the books which deal specifically with this class of work. The specimens which I offer here in illustration of the subject are taken from less known buildings, and are chosen for their simplicity of style—there is nothing aggressively Jacobean or Elizabethan about them. They have no strong reminiscences of Gothic tradition, still less do they breathe the spirit of the New Birth. They are quiet evidences of straightforward Anglo-Saxon construction in a

Front View
Fig. 3. RAWLINSON FARM, ROLVENDEN, KENT

plain, honest Anglo-Saxon material. They are *homes* in fact. And whatever there is about them of style is of that style which is merely the outcome of direct expression in handicraft. It is the style of the bench, not that of the study. They show craftsmanship, not scholarship. One of my illustrations, that of Godfrey House, Hollingbourne, has an ascertained date. It was erected in 1587, and, strangely enough, has survived without hopeless disfigurement a restoration in 1859, a date at which restoration could still be unkind. This photograph with that of Wesley's cottage at Rolvenden Layne (Kent), exhibit the use of diagonal struts in the framing, which in some examples is found strongly developed, and in others is purposely, as far as possible, suppressed. Obviously there are conditions under which diagonals of this kind are a great source of strength in a construction which without them might succumb disastrously to oblique pressure, but it is a curious fact that rural builders, who cultivated this picturesque method, were sometimes very unmethodical in their disposition of these elements of stability,

and appear to have used at random what one thinks should be a calculated force in the structural economy.

The two views (Figs. 3 and 4) of Rawlinson Farm, Rolvenden (Kent), give an example of the *vertical* method undisturbed by any diagonal features of design. Brick is, of course, employed for the chimneys in all these constructions and in the last example is even made use of for some of the walling, but the constructors have evidently felt that for general purposes the claims both of beauty and economy demanded the use of timber. The cottage at Martyr Worthing (Fig. 5), a very humble little building, leads to the mention of a second method of filling-in between the posts of the framework—the use, namely, of brickwork itself as a sort of subsidiary. This method is a strange reversal of our modern methods and modern ideas. The architect of today, who uses his half-timber work for its visible effect rather than for any constructional value, is wont, in England at least, to plant his timber framing (sometimes rather thin framing, too) upon a backwork of brick, thereby acknowledging to himself at least, if not

Rear View
Fig. 4. RAWLINSON FARM, ROLVENDEN, KENT

to his public, that he looks to the brick for stability, warmth and resistance to weather, and recognizes the wooden formation as a merely aesthetic adjunct. With the older generation the motif was reversed. Brick was well enough for a mere filling-in, but the strength was expected from the timber.

Another cottage (Fig. 6) exhibits yet another method of finishing the surface of a timber-built wall. The upper story is so plastered and colored as to produce the appearance of a uniform material. The plaster-work of the filling-in between the beams is either quite flush with the face of the timber (as in the left-hand portion of the building) or is brought so far forward, as in the right-hand gable, that the lath-work and rendering are carried right over the face of the wooden posts. In this example will be seen an instance of the device common to most European town architecture of wooden construction, the corbelling-out of the upper story in advance of that below. There are many good reasons for this expedient, and its method of construction is extremely simple. It will be understood that the carrying over of the upper wall-surfaces

not only provides a shelter for passengers on the pavement, but is a great protection to the building itself. In any building in which such a treatment is applied to one story above another in several stages, it is obvious that the foundations are completely protected from drip, and that each stage is shielded from wet by the stage above it. Another advantage where land is valuable is that, while observing the frontage line at the street level, the owner gains a little added accommodation by enlarging his site, so to speak, at the upper levels. Needless to say, the vestries, borough councils and district-surveyors of modern cities are very chary of permitting such old-time methods of overhead trespass.

The simplest method of effecting an overhanging wall of this description is to carry the floor-joists through the front wall, allowing them to project to the required distance. On the end of these joists, which thus become cantilevers, is placed the wooden framing which forms the front wall of the upper story, neatly finished off with a moulded fascia.

One of the noteworthy facts in the history of English

Fig. 5. COTTAGE AT MARTYR WORTHING,
NEAR WINCHESTER, HANTS

timber architecture is that, in spite of all the changes of passing styles and fashions, almost in opposition to them, it pursued its course as a natural vernacular and traditional craft, and thus retained a continuity unknown to the kindred arts of masonry and brickwork. The carpenter had a soul above foreign novelties, or, to put it more simply and, perhaps, more truthfully, he had about him a good British obstinacy, which retarded the growth of innovation and kept alive the spirit of antiquity in his handiwork. Mr. Blomfield, in his *History of the Renaissance in England,* gives full prominence to this important factor in the architectural developments of our country. "The earlier examples of sixteenth-century carpentry are," he says, "Gothic rather than Renaissance in character. The old methods in use by the excellent carpenters of the fifteenth century were regularly followed, and the gables, the over-hanging stories, the spurs or angle-posts, cusping and tracery, and many a detail of ornamentation show that, in spite of the changes that were imminent, the carpenter followed the mediaeval tradition as faithfully as his inferior skill would allow, and

few things are more remarkable in the history of English art than the pertinacity of this tradition."

The whole of the Elizabethan and Jacobean periods of English architecture must have been full of manifestations of street architecture exhibiting the principles of construction with which I have been dealing and the spirit of traditional conservatism to which Mr. Blomfield alludes. Thanks to an almost divine protection which has saved many of these beautiful fabrics from the destruction which might have seemed almost inevitable, it would be possible still to illustrate this part of the subject with a very large collection of reproductions from buildings still in existence. The few photographs here brought together will be enough for our immediate purpose. Five of my examples (Figs. 7, 8, 9, 10, 11) are from Dartmouth, a town which rivals Chester in its devices for obtaining the maximum amount of house-room over the pavement, and like Chester, though in a less degree, secures the result by the erection of a colonnade above the sidewalk, thereby producing a covered way. The houses in the Butter Walk (Figs. 7 and 10) belong, I suppose, to the middle of the

Fig. 6. HOUSE AT WEST WYCOMBE, BUCKS

Fig. 7. THE BUTTER WALK, DARTMOUTH

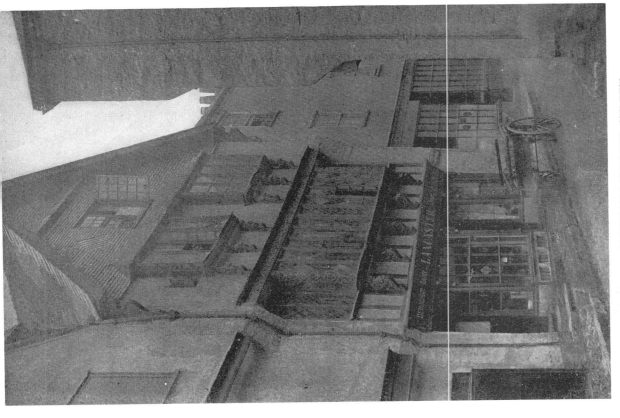

Fig. 8. OLD HOUSE IN HOOPER STREET, DARTMOUTH

Fig. 9. DETAIL OF WINDOW IN THE BUTTER WALK, DARTMOUTH

Fig. 10. THE BUTTER WALK, DARTMOUTH

seventeenth century, and are certainly brilliant examples of an architecture the style of which is much more easily defined by geographical than by chronological limits. Its genius, one may say, is Gothic: it is of a piece with the traditions of that older England to which the whisper of the Italian awakening had not yet come; nor can it be said that, while Gothic in structure, it is Classic in detail: certainly it offers here and there a passable "guilloche," and there is a hint in places of a dentil-course and a regulation beaded astragal, but the closer one looks the less evidence one finds of the proprieties of scholarship. That twining-vine of the first-floor frieze has about it an archaic freedom that might grow upon an "ambo" at Torcello, and the uncouth slab that surmounts the columns (who shall dub them Doric?) is far more like the rude energy of Ravenna than any example to be found in the handbooks of Palladio or in the *Mirror of Architecture*. The sashes which have found their way into the top story and into the sides of the bay window are, of course, interpolations, little bits of innovation already grown

old. The two further Dartmouth examples (Figs. 8 and 11) are evidently of the same period. They exhibit the same excellence of carving in the corbels which support the bay windows, proof of the fact, which is sometimes overlooked, that alongside of an almost barbaric habit of sculpture in frieze-work and running ornament there existed in England, throughout the seventeenth and eighteenth centuries, a school of architectural carvers whose work had all the elements of rustic vigor and beauty.

The West of England must have been especially rich in timber street-architecture. Even in Bristol, a town which is becoming rapidly modernized, there are side streets close to the main thoroughfares that set one thinking of Shakespeare, and Exeter, a city not yet absorbed by the enterprise of the latter-day commerce, contains several houses of ancient date. The simpler of my two examples (Fig. 12) is a good specimen of that bow-window treatment, coupled with overhanging stories, which gains for the owner increased accommodation on each higher floor; and the same thing is

Fig. 11. HOUSE AT DARTMOUTH

Fig. 12. TWO HOUSES IN THE HIGH STREET, EXETER

exhibited in Figure 13, which I take to be a somewhat older house.

To turn from Western England to Kent, we see once more what can be done with timber, and how long it may endure in the two examples which I have taken from Rochester. The designer of the house in Figure 14 must, I think, have produced an internal effect which it might be worthwhile to repeat in modern buildings. There has been in modern England a strife of architects over the subject of the function of windows, one extreme school holding that as the use of a window is to let in light, it is well to range the windows at a high level along the whole length of the window wall, the other arguing that the window's mission is to give the inhabitant the means of looking out, and that, therefore, the sill must be placed so low down that the eye even of a person sitting well back in the room is not obstructed in its outward vision; a middle school, containing most persons of common sense, has realized that the window has, and always has had, both functions, and has, therefore, perpetuated the use of the

ordinary normal window, which, while keeping a low sill, gets what effect of breadth it can, without unduly absorbing the wall space. I think that this Rochester window would unite the demands of both disputant parties, not by the concessions of compromise (which imply a sacrifice on both sides, but by positively uniting the claims of both systems). In the other Rochester house (Fig. 15) we may admire the bravery which has abandoned symmetry. We have here an elevation marked out by three gables; beneath them on both first and second floors are three bay windows, but the designer thinking more of inward convenience than outward effect, or, perhaps, realizing, as few men realize in these days of drawing boards, that a building in a street is not often seen in true orthographic elevation, has thrown his center-lines to the winds and produced a composition whose grace is no way marred by the neglect of vertical rhythm.

These instances will have given point to the quotation from Mr. Blomfield's book, and will have shown how it came about that the development which we

Fig. 13. OLD HOUSES IN THE HIGH STREET,
EXETER

Fig. 14. EASTGATE HOUSE, ROCHESTER, KENT

Fig. 15. HOUSES IN ROCHESTER, KENT

Fig. 16. CLOTH HALL, NEWBURY

Fig. 17. *Brackets* — CLOTH HALL, NEWBURY

know as Georgian architecture found the English builders steeped in the living traditions of centuries of timber-construction. The importance of this as a factor in the success of that architecture will be easily demonstrated. Meanwhile, before turning into the Georgian period, let me offer just one more example of earlier work, the rather nondescript but certainly picturesque little Cloth Hall at Newbury, which, at the time of writing, is about to be saved from ruin by a careful reparation. One would hardly guess from a first glance at the illustration (Fig. 16) how largely the building partakes of wooden construction. A coating of cement has reduced the whole of the upper story to an appearance of uniform material; but it becomes obvious as one studies the way in which that upper story is supported that though the endwall, with its stone coping and solid "kneelers," is probably of brickwork, the side walls, supported as they are by the wooden brackets shown in Figure 17 (and no doubt by concealed floor-joists as well), must, undoubtedly, be of wooden framing.[1] The very base-wall, which the failure of the cement-facing reveals to be brick, is not of brick alone, but has a skeleton of timber, and I doubt not that the Doric columns (whose round abaci suggest the misinterpretation of a drawing) are of really constructive value. I suspect that the cement labels are a modern addition.

There are many folks to whom it occurs to think that

[1] I have confirmed this impression by examining one of the walls since I wrote these remarks. The side wall is of timber-framing, battened, hung with tiles and rendered with cement above the tiles.

Georgian architecture consists of a rather meaningless addition of scraps of Classical reminiscence to an otherwise rather commonplace method of house-building. They would tell you that the recipe for such Art was simply to design your building as nearly as possible in the form of a cube; to place your doors and windows as symmetrically as may be; to trim the latter with lengths of so-called architrave moulding; to deck the door with a flattened composition which might be a direct transcript from anybody's book on the Roman orders; to apply to the eaves any Classic cornice that happens to be adaptable, and to confine the internal decoration to the perpetration of yet one more theft from the architectural class-books, a set of chimney-pieces which shall be mimic representations of the temple ruins in the Forum, and, in the United States, to paint the wooden walls yellow and the standing-finish white.

Now, a very little thought and a very little study will show the unreasonableness of this taunt; and there may be no harm in going for a while to the root of the matter. However much we may laugh at the theorists who see in every detail of Classic architecture the survival of some feature or other in a prehistoric wooden construction, there can, I think, be no question but that there must be *some* truth in the idea that the orders and their adjuncts are derived from wooden tradition. Obviously, wood preceded stone as the primitive material of human habitations. Obviously, a timber log makes a better and a longer beam than does a stone lintel; obviously, under certain circumstances, a vertical trunk makes as good a post or

Fig. 18. HOUSE AT TOTNES, SOUTH DEVON

Fig. 19. HOUSE ON THE ABBEY YARD, BATH

column as can be made out of stone. In fact, from the point-of-view of primitive man, and for the purpose of immediate needs, setting aside durability and permanence, wood is as useful a material for building as stone. We are, therefore, almost bound to look for a timber architecture as the logical and historical predecessor of architecture in stone, and, indeed, the more that study is given to the functional nature of the detail of the Classic orders the more does it become apparent that the shapes which have become so fixed and familiar can claim a reasonable derivation in wooden forms. Even if such a parentage be disproved, the converse of my argument is, undoubtedly, true, and it is this converse truth that I am here at pains to set forth. Perhaps the very best instance in point is that of the eighteenth-century application of the Classic cornice as the crowning-member of a Georgian gentleman's house. What did necessity demand? A gutter, a covering for the heels of the rafters, and some collection of mouldings of receding section, which would effect the required amount of projection from wall-face to gutter, without allowing overflow from the gutter to run down the wall-face. All these requirements you may fulfill without great expense, and with a good deal of refinement, by simply working in deal the regulation mouldings of the Tuscan, Doric, Ionic, or Corinthian order. The cyma, whether you execute it in lead-lined wood or in metal, will give you your gutter, the fascia covers your rafter-heels, and the bed-mould, with or without trusses, according to the amount of projection required, neatly finishes, and partly supports, the whole arrangement in a way which precludes the dribbling of water down the frontage.

So, again, with the Georgian porch. The house-builder says to himself—"My walls are of brick and they are 14 or, may be, 18 inches thick. I cannot, for various reasons, form my doorway of entrance simply by making an aperture of 7 feet by 3 feet through the wall, with a door hung in it. For one thing, brick is an unpleasant material to rub against in coming into the house, for another I want more depth than my 14 or 18 inches will give me, so that a waiting visitor on the doorstep may have some protection from sun and rain. To secure this I must apply wood or some such material to my reveals, and I must contrive to bring this construction forward so as to stand in advance of the general wall-face, and so increase the shelter. Now, my projecting pattern must be roofed-in within something that slopes conveniently to right and left; there must, moreover, be no sharp angles about the projecting jambs of my shelter, and if I can get a semicircular fanlight over my door so much the better."

As it happens, every one of these many conditions is fulfilled, and with scarcely an ounce of unnecessary material, by the severely Classical design which makes the elegant doorway shown in Figure 20. The ovolo-moulded paneling neatly clothes the jambs of the brick opening, the columns provide a rounded surface at the very spot where angularity must be avoided, they also produce by their projection from the general wall-face the additional depth of reveal required for additional shelter, and they carry as their crowning-feature a Roman pediment, whose lines present the very outline most convenient for discharge of rain-water. As a final touch of convenience it will be noted that the fragment of frieze and architrave between capital and cornice, so far from being a mere concession to Classical etiquette, offers just the amount of extra height required to make possible the insertion of a legitimate semicircular arch, which besides its legitimacy has the merit of supplying the one remaining want—a glimmer of light for the hall. The useful, they say, is synonymous with the beautiful. Here is a composition which fulfills a set of wants in every particular. On this account it is, philosophically speaking, a thing of beauty; but, besides being this, it satisfies the minutest requirements of the Classical amateur. It is, therefore, doubly admirable; trebly, I might even say, for who will deny its claim to beauty on other and less secondary grounds.

To what extent the genius of this Georgian architecture was a timber genius may be seen by comparing my examples numbered 18 and 19. The latter represents a house in Bath, the Ionic frontage of which is executed not in wood, but in the celebrated Bath stone, but the former—a street-house in Totnes (South Devon)—is, I believe, erected entirely in wood. It is a rather curious fact that by an accident of selection both these examples do violence to the architectural canon that a columnar composition should have as its center a void and not a solid. One is a group of three pilasters, the other one of five, but in spite of this fault, which to many eyes is a fault rather academic than real, it will be owned that both examples exhibit propriety and grace. To be quite honest one must acknowledge that the order and entablature in the case of the Bath house is merely ornamental, though even here one might plead that the cornice protects the wall, and that the pilasters which support it are little more than the legitimate application of ornament to the piers between the windows. In the Devonshire specimen the cornice has an added function, for it conveys across the frontage with considerable *aplomb* the transverse gutter, which would otherwise be a serious disfigurement of the aspect of the house. But my point in thus offering these two illustrations is that the use of the order and entablature which, in its stone treatment at Bath is a perfectly reasonable, commonsense, and beautiful

Fig. 20. DOORWAY AT NEWTON ABBOTT

Fig. 22. DOORWAY NEAR GOUDHURST, KENT

Fig. 21. DOORWAY AT DARTMOUTH

Fig. 23. DOORWAY AT DORKING

employment of an Italian *motif* evolved from Roman antiquity, is in its wooden development at Totnes equally happy, equally congruous, and equally true. It is, in fact, still architecture and not mere decoration nor mere archaeology.

Sometimes the Classicism of a Georgian house is so entirely coextensive with its joinery that the two seem almost synonymous. You may find a house the fabric of which is mainly brick, showing wherever it shows timber the culture of the Renaissance. Here are two graceful eighteenth-century door heads, which illustrate such a tendency, the one[2] is from Bristol, the other (Fig. 21) from Dartmouth. The shell in the former, which became so favorite a feature during the Georgian period, is, of course, no transcript of antiquity, but is a development, and a perfectly reasonable, logical and suitable development from Classic and Renaissance ideas. It is legitimate design within the limits and under the genius of the adopted style. The happy evolution of such a feature is the kind of thing that serves to prove to those who balance inventive art against antiquarian, that architects can be at one and the same time conservative and progressive. Of the corbels which support the shellhead, one might say that they are lawful descendants of the Corinthian modillion. The modillion's projection and depth have certainly been increased at the expense of its other dimension, but there are sound structural reasons for such a change, and the result, instead of striking the beholder as a travesty on antiquity, appeals to him at once as being an adaptation of an ancient feature to modern needs, without loss of beauty, without loss of the charms of traditional association. The Dartmouth door (Fig. 22), that bears its date so bravely, is a simpler thing, nearer to type in some ways, farther from it in others. The use of the curved pediment is, of course, the adoption of the variation which the Italian architects introduced; as for the mouldings, every one of them has its Classic ancestor, but the brackets or corbels are of an essentially British type. Brackets of closely similar design are extremely common all through England, and their origin, if ones comes to look for it, is fairly obvious. This familiar form is nothing more, or less, than a representation in outline (without detail) of the Corinthian modillion, *including* its foliage. Under ordinary circumstances, it would occur to most designers that if the carving of the modillion were too expensive for his present requirements, the natural course would be to use the scroll or volute element of the modillion or truss without the leafage, but this idea did not satisfy some of the car-

penters of Georgian England, who preferred to cut out of board a figure which should be capable of at least casting a shadow similar to the grander article which expense forbade.

And now I am brought to my final examples, which will show, certainly in rather a humble way, how the simplest form of rural wood-architecture was able to carry with grace the ornaments and, to a large extent, the spirit of the gracious style of which we are treating here. In Figures 22 and 23, one may see English wood-construction of the simplest type—a building whose timber-frame is outwardly protected by clapboards, or, as we generally call them in England, "weather-boards." Such cottages abound in parts of Kent to the present day, and their inhabitants are ready to vouch for their warmth and dryness. How, it may be asked, can architecture of this description lend itself without incongruity to the assumption of the Classical elegancies of Georgian building-craft? The answer, I suppose, is found even more readily in American Colonial architecture than in the houses of England; but we have our examples, too, and the little and unpretentious dwelling near Goudhurst will serve to give proof to the main argument of this short essay, which is, to express it briefly, that the Classicism of Georgian architecture, its art, in fact, was intimately and congenially associated with wood as a building material. The Englishman's love for timber had not always had free rein. There was a check at the end of the sixteenth century, a sort of timber panic. Twice, at least, official reports were made to the officers of the Crown on the excessive consumption of timber in the Southern counties (chiefly in the iron-mills) and it is believed that the regulation which followed this report led to the suppression of half-timber work in the Southern districts. Certain it is that the forests of England had been making, even in the course of a hundred years, alarming progress towards disappearance, and there was thought to be some ground for the fear that ship-building might be in danger. But a century later, these anxieties would seem to have abated. Half-timber, which generally implies oak, was, indeed, no more; brick was more largely adopted as the material of walls; but it is a fact that those very districts of Surrey, Kent and Sussex, in which the wood panic had occurred, contain more examples than most parts of the country of the use of timber-fronts in Georgian work. Two new causes may have been already in operation, the importation of timber and the disuse of the South country ironworks.

I think that the house-carpenter has somehow lacked a poet to sing his praises, and even historians have rather allowed him to be overshadowed by the mysterious mason. There can be little doubt that for

---

[2]This cut, we regret to say, has been lost by the plate-maker, but as a substitute we will refer to the shell-hoods shown on pages 64–65 and 66. — WARE

OLD HOUSE, FARMINGTON, CONNECTICUT

centuries the carpenter was, in England, the great transmitter of tradition, the great artist in construction, and a contriver of so high an order as to merit the name of designer. He was a great man in Gothic times; he was a great man still in Renaissance and Georgian times, and whereas the mason undoubtedly changed his *personnel,* occasionally being at one period and another a foreigner, introduced to carry out the new ideas from the Continent, whether Italian or Dutch, I expect that our friend the carpenter must have endured much less of foreign substitution; with the versatility of his craft he lent himself easily to the new modes (which were, in truth, such old ones), and found with all the joy of an artist that these cymas and ovolos, flutes and astragals were the very things his tools were meant to work. He was without more ado at home with these bits of Rome and Greece. He worked, he prospered, and became the backbone of Georgian art.

IT would be very easy to show the justness of Mr. Waterhouse's line of reasoning by a reference to the work of the seventeenth-century carpenter in this country, for some of the still extant buildings built from 1640 onwards show unmistakable evidence of the work of English carpenters, who had, of course, not yet felt the impulse of the Classic movement of the time of Anne and the Georges, but merely followed on new soil the traditions of English carpentry handed down from the times of the Gothic masters of the art.

Half-timber work, pure and simple, was probably little used: wood was at hand, but bricks were not, and by the time native brickyards were in operation the practice of all-wood construction had become commonly understood and habitual. Still, there is a kind of reminiscence of half-timbering in the brick-nogged wall so commonly used for the north and east walls of old New England houses, though, as the outer face is covered with clapboards, like the other walls of the house, while the inner face is concealed behind lath and plaster, the presence of brickwork is no more suspected by most observers than it was in the case of the Cloth Hall at Newbury mentioned above.

In still another particular was English practice repeated in American houses, and though here no restricted site made it desirable for a builder to gain space in the upper stories by making them overhang the walls of the story below, yet the practice was very generally followed, and we have houses like the Whip-

ple House, at Ipswich, Massachusetts, and the Waller House, at Salem, for instance, where the upper story overhangs the lower, more or less. The explanation is, simply, that the house-builders here followed the method of framing—a very logical method—to which they had been habituated in England. It has been very common to consider these overhangs as a recession from and modification of a custom that certainly did prevail in the early block-houses and some of the semi-fortified dwellings where a considerable overhang was purposely given to the upper story, so that the door and window openings in the lower walls might be commanded through loopholes in the projecting part of the upper floor. Many an observer, haunted by a schoolboy belief that all overhanging floors were signs of former Indian strife, has vainly tried to understand how loopholes cut in such slight projections could ever have commanded any savage standing close against the wall below: others, thinking themselves more intelligent perhaps, saw in these peculiarities of construction only another evidence of the universal conservatism of mankind, and smiled at the seeming unwillingness of the builders to confess in their work that, since Indian onslaught was no longer to be feared, there was no longer need to even indicate an overhang which had become abbreviated by atrophy. It took the patient examination that Messrs. Isham and Brown gave to the old buildings of the seventeenth century to make it quite plain that in most cases these overhangs had nothing to do with Indian warfare, but were simply and frankly the expression of the method of framing employed by the early carpenters, and Mr. Waterhouse, above, shows clearly that these early builders of ours were not inventing new methods of framing, but simply following those which were familiar to them from their apprentice days at home.

Although the seventeenth-century buildings have not perhaps as much architectural character as those of the Georgian period they are vastly interesting and picturesque, and, for one thing, afford an unrivalled chance for studying the effect of roof-lines. There are so many ways in which a study of these old buildings can be made useful that it is worth while to give below an incomplete list of seventeenth-century buildings still extant in Massachusetts, and a few elsewhere, compiled from sundry recent contributions under "Notes and Queries" of the Boston *Transcript*. We give the list for what it is worth, having made no attempt to verify name, date (which sometimes differs from that stated elsewhere in this work) or actual present existence of the structures enumerated. In all probability, many of the buildings have only their age to recommend them to notice. — WARE

WALLER HOUSE — 1684 — ST. PETER'S STREET, SALEM, MASSACHUSETTS

MARIA GOODHUE HOUSE, DANVERS, MASSACHUSETTS

Amesbury, Massachusetts:
  Macy House 1654
Andover, Massachusetts:
  Abbott House 1690
  Bradstreet House, Gov . .1667
  Holt House 1675
Arlington, Massachusetts:
  Locke House, Abel . . .1690 or
    1719
  Locke House, W . .1684 or 1760
  Russell House 1680
Bedford, Massachusetts:
  Bacon House 1682
Beverly, Massachusetts:
  Baker House 1685
  Conant House . . . . . . .16 —
  Trask House 1692
Billerica, Massachusetts:
  Fletcher House 1650
Boston, Massachusetts:
  Charter Street, No 23 . .1694
  Greenough Lane and
    Vernon Place 1698
  Hancock Tavern 1634
  Mather House, Cotton . . .1677
  Revere House, Paul 1678
  Sun Tavern 1690
  Tremere House 1674
  Wells House 1660
Bourne, Massachusetts:
  Bourne House . . . . .16 —
Brookline, Massachusetts:
  Aspinwall House 1660
  Devotion House . . . . . .16 —
Burlington, Massachusetts:
  Cutler House 1650
  Reed-Wyman House 1665
Cambridge, Massachusetts:
  Austin House 1666
  Bishop's Palace,
    Linden Ave. . . . . .16 —
  Lee House, Judge

Joseph 1680
Chelsea, Massachusetts:
  Bellingham House, Gov. .1670
  Cary House 1660
  Pratt House 1670
Chestnut Hill, Massachusetts:
  Hammond House 1640
  Kingsbury House 1700
Concord, Massachusetts:
  Barrett House,
    Col. James 1660
  Hunt-Hosmer House 1680
  Tavern . . . . —
Danvers, Massachusetts:
  Clarke House, Joseph P . .1650
  Endicott House 1675
  Fowler House 1634
  Harris House 1650
  Houlton House 1650
  Jacobs House 1658
  Jacobs (Witch) House,
    George 1650
  Osborn House, Sarah . . .1660
  Page House . . . . .16 —
  Prince House 1660
  Putnam-Goodhue House .1650
  Townsend-Bishop-Nourse
    House 1636
Dedham, Massachusetts:
  Fairbanks House 1640
  White House, Cedar St. .1648
Dorchester, Massachusetts:
  Blake House 1640
  Bridgham House 1635
  Capen House, Barnard . .1628
  Clap House, Roger 1640
  Mattapan Road House . .1690
  Pierce House, Robert 1635
Duxbury, Massachusetts:
  Alden House, John 1653
  Standish House, Myles . .1666
East Braintree, Massachusetts:
  Wales House, Elder 1681

East Wareham, Massachusetts:
  Gibbs House . . . . .16 —
*Framingham Center,
  Massachusetts:*
  Haven House 1694

Gloucester, Massachusetts:
  Sawyer House . . . . .16 —
Greenland, New Hampshire:
  Old Brick House 1638
Guilford, Connecticut:
  Garrison-Whitfield House
    (Old Stone) 1635
Haverhill, Massachusetts:
  Peaslee-Garrison House . .1670
  Whittier's Birthplace 1690
Hingham, Massachusetts:
  Cushing House 1679
  Gay House, Parson 1680
  Jacobs House, Nicholas . .1675
  Lincoln House, General .1650
  Meeting House,
    Old Ship 1680

Ipswich, Massachusetts:
  Bond House 1633
  Caldwell House 1640
  Dodge House 1640
  Howard-Emerson House .1675
  Jones House, William . .1726
  Norton-Corbett House . .1660
  Sutton House 1642
  Whipple House 1635
  Whittlesey House 1640
  Winthrop House 1634
Kingston, Massachusetts:
  Bradford House, Major . .1675
  Cobb House 1640
  Cushman House 1680
  Willett House 1638
Kittery, Maine:
  Bray House 1660

Lexington, Massachusetts:
  Bowman House 1649
  Buckman Tavern 1690
  Estabrook House, Rev. B .1693
  Hancock House 1698
  Munroe Tavern . .1675 or 1695
  Plummer House 1693
Lowell, Massachusetts:
  Clerk House 1670
  Dracut-Gavin House . . . .16 —
Lunenburg, Massachusetts:
  Cushing House . . . . . . .16 —
Marblehead, Massachusetts:
  Doak House 1675
  Tucker House, Old 1640
Marshfield, Massachusetts:
  Winslow House 1642
Medfield, Massachusetts:
  Clark House 1680
Medford, Massachusetts:
  Barrack, Old 1650
  Cradock Fort 1634
  Cradock-Wellington
    House 1636
Melrose, Massachusetts:
  Lynde House 1675
Milton, Massachusetts:
  Houghton House 1680
  Tucker House 1643
Nantucket, Massachusetts:
  Coffin House 1680
  Meader House, Hannah .16 —
  Paddock House 1675
Newbury, Massachusetts:
  Coffin House, Tristram . .1652
  Donahue House 1640
  Hale House 1650
  Ilsley House 1670
  Noyes House, Parson 1645
  Sexton-Short House 1700
  Spencer-Pierce House . . .1650
  Toppan House 1670

CORBETT HOUSE — 1635 — IPSWICH,
MASSACHUSETTS

SALTONSTALL HOUSE — 1635 — IPSWICH,
MASSACHUSETTS

SHEDD HOUSE—1680—BRIGHTON,
MASSACHUSETTS

BOARDMAN HOUSE—1700—SAUGUS,
MASSACHUSETTS

Newcastle, New Hampshire:
Jaffrey-Albee House 1675
Newport, Rhode Island:
Arnold's Mill, Benedict . . 1666
Bull House, Henry 1639
Friends Meeting House . . 1700
North Andover, Massachusetts:
Bradstreet House 1667
Peabody, Massachusetts:
Buxton House 1680
Goodale House . . . . 16—
Needham House 1665
Pope House . . . . 16—
Pembroke, Massachusetts:
Barker House, Old 1640
Plymouth, Massachusetts:
Doten House 1660
Harlow House 1675
Howland-Carver House . . 1666
Morton-Whiting House . . 1667
Portsmouth, New Hampshire:
Crowe House 1680

Jackson House 1660
Quincy, Massachusetts:
Adams House 1681
Quincy-Butler House . . . 1680
Revere, Massachusetts:
Newgate-Yeaman
House 1650
Roxbury, Massachusetts:
Walker-Williams House . 1680

Salem, Massachusetts:
Bakery, Old 1690
First Church 1631
Hawthorne's Birthplace . . 1675
Pickering House 1650
Shattuck Witch House . . 1675
Turner House
(of Seven Gables) 1666
Waller-Ward House 1690
Williams (Witch) House,
Roger 1635
Salisbury, Massachusetts:
Osgood House 1646

Saugus, Massachusetts:
Hill-Boardman House . . . 1650
Old Iron Works 1643
Scituate, Massachusetts:
Otis House 1680
Scituate Harbor, Massachusetts:
Baker House 1634
Somerville, Massachusetts:
Somerville Ave., No. 478 . 1690
Sudbury, Massachusetts:
Walker-Garrison House . 1660
Wayside Inn 1680
Swampscott, Massachusetts:
Blaney House 1640
Mudge House 1634

Topsfield, Massachusetts:
Andrews House 1685
Capen-Garrison House . . 1660

Waban, Massachusetts:
Woodward Homestead . . 1686

Watertown, Massachusetts:
Brown House 1633
Wenham, Massachusetts:
Ober House 1680
*West Bridgewater,
Massachusetts:*
Keith House 1662
Westwood, Massachusetts:
Colburn House 1650
Winthrop, Massachusetts:
Bill House 1650
Deane Winthrop House . 1649
Woburn, Massachusetts:
Baldwin House 1681
Cutler House 1690

York, Maine:
Jail 1653
Mackintire Garrison
House 1645
Moulton House 1675

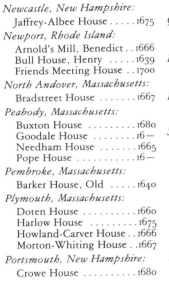

SARAH OSBORN HOUSE—c1690—DANVERS,
MASSACHUSETTS

GEORGE JACOBS (WITCH) HOUSE—1690—
DANVERSPORT, MASSACHUSETTS[1]

MILLS-WARD HOUSE, SALEM,
MASSACHUSETTS[1]

[1] After photographs by Frank Cousins, Salem, Massachusetts

KING MANOR HOUSE

The King Manor House, now owned by the town of Jamaica, Long Island, and leased to an association of ladies for care and preservation, was built in 1805 by Rufus King as an enlargement of an older portion (still extant) built by Ames Smith in 1750.

MONTICELLO

Although Mr. Skinner elsewhere gives the date of Monticello as 1810, other authorities say that it was begun in 1764, and that when Mr. Jefferson brought his bride home to Monticello in 1772, it was to a fully completed house that he brought her.

COTTAGES, BATTLE, SUSSEX, ENGLAND

Detail of Mantelpiece
GREAT WIGSELL, SUSSEX, ENGLAND

Detail of Mantel
GREAT WIGSELL, SUSSEX, ENGLAND

Detail of Mantelpiece
MAYOR'S PARLOR IN THE TOWN HALL, SOUTH MOULTON, ENGLAND

·Old·Fireplaces

·Bristol

·No·

·E·P·M·

5   6   7 *ft.*

Dighton·St·

Eng·

1·

·After measured drawings· by· E·G· Rodway·

·Scale·

1 2 3

·Old·Fireplaces·

·Bristol·

·No·

·E·P·M·

Dighton · St ·

Eng ·

2 ·

·After·measured· drawings· by · E · G · Rodway ·

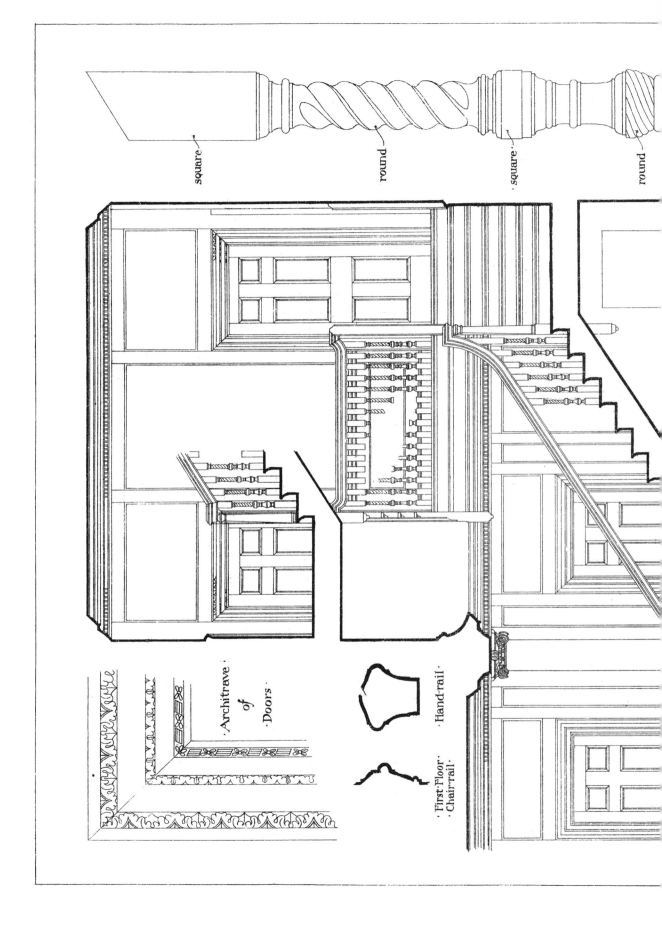

square

round

square

round

Architrave
of
Doors

Hand-rail

First-Floor
Chair-rail

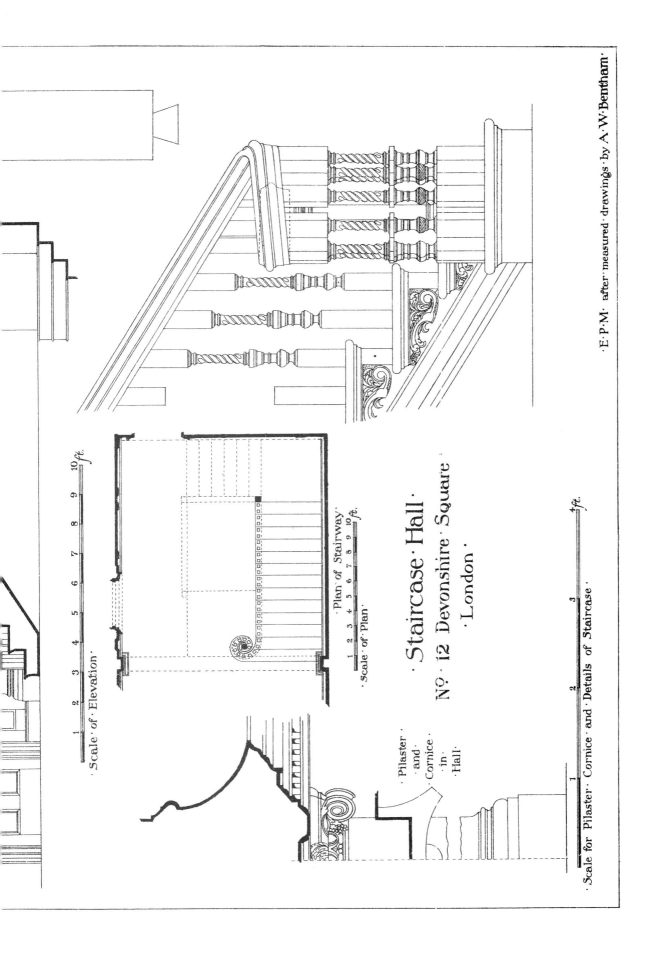

· Scale · of · Elevation ·

· Plan · of · Stairway ·

· Scale · of · Plan ·

· Staircase · Hall ·

Nº · 12 · Devonshire · Square ·
· London ·

· Pilaster ·
· and ·
· Cornice ·
· in ·
· Hall ·

· Scale · for · Pilaster · Cornice · and · Details · of · Staircase ·

· E · P · M · after · measured · drawings · by · A · W · Bentham ·

HOUSE NEAR GOUDHURST, KENT, ENGLAND

Georgian Door Heads
in London

Text by
Owen Fleming
Originally published in 1900 as
Volume II of The Georgian Period

Fig. 8. QUEEN ANNE'S GATE,
WESTMINSTER, S. W.

GEORGIAN DOOR HEADS IN LONDON

THE London door heads illustrated in this chapter are typical of seventeenth and eighteenth century work and are probably chiefly interesting as regarded comparatively, and as evidence of the spirit of the times which produced them. Additional importance however is found in the fact that these examples of ancient work become year by year scarcer, disappearing for the most part into the yard of the indiscriminating house-breaker, and but rarely preserved in appreciation of merit. As architectural features belonging to a time singularly barren as regards London exteriors, they possess a significance generically, which, developed to however extreme degree in modern architecture, is ample in itself. Of late years, when nothing is so characteristic of modern architecture as freedom from traditional restraint, nor anything so notable as the evidences of loving study and admiration of the time-spirit moving in the sixteenth and seventeenth centuries, it would probably be interesting to note the play of fancy given to the reproduction of this feature — the doorway. It is indeed interesting, but there is one restriction which breaks the entirety of the development — the present building-regulation, which now forbids the erection of such a feature in wood. The restriction has been met in many ways — by the employment of carved brick, stone, stucco and, more recently and with considerable success, terracotta. Wood, however, is a material with characteristic limitations and peculiarities entirely foreign to all these substitutes; so the door head as here illustrated has, so far as London is concerned, come to be a relic of the past, not to be reproduced, save to the arbitrary

satisfaction of the district-surveyors. At any rate, work of this nature is never carried out in London now.

It is curious to note that in London domestic work of the period under discussion, the seventeenth and eighteenth centuries, practically the whole of the external decorative work was concentrated in the doorway and its approach, the iron-railed threshold. Walling, windows, and for the most part the area railings, were plain and simple in the extreme. Only the actual doorway and the threshold railings, the iron lamp brackets and link-extinguisher were wrought with some generosity of spirit. The magnification of the entry has of course a prime importance architecturally; and into this perception the sixteenth and seventeenth century builders entered fully.

There are still remaining in the older parts of London streets and courts with door heads in profusion, but for the most part examples occur in partial solitude, where chance combination of circumstance has permitted of preservation. Particularly in mind at this moment are the districts of the Adelphi, Westminster, Bloomsbury, Chelsea, and the lanes and streets neighboring the various Inns of Court. Deptford, too, south of the Thames, for centuries important as a shipping and ship-building center, is rich in door heads; when we remember that this was the English home of Grinling Gibbons, the master woodcarver of English Renaissance, it is easy to conceive that a genius that stamped itself in every cut of the tool, would be an influence spreading from whatever centers contained his most notable work. In the City and East End examples are not wanting where, a century ago, the mer-

Fig. 1.   CHEYNE ROW, CHELSEA, S. W.

chant lived with his work and had not been steam-taught to sleep ten, twenty—fifty miles from his ledger.

To consider the sketches here shown; those from Buckingham Street, Adelphi (Figs. 3 and 5), from their similarities somewhat naturally fall together. Features, as they are, of houses of equal date, of one building scheme, they have so much in common as to lead to the belief, on external evidence, that they are the work of one mind. Buckingham Street was formed, according to Pepys's *Diary*, somewhere between 1660 and 1684; the old York House, which occupied the site, was then destroyed and residences named "York Buildings" erected on the site. Part of these houses have been rebuilt, but the original construction was so recent that there can be little hesitation in deciding if the original has or has not been preserved; and with regard to the two houses from which these sketches (Figs. 3 and 5) are made, there is every reason to attach to them as date that of the original construction. The date, therefore, of the work

in these heads may be stated to be the end of the seventeenth century. It is known that Wren was *persona grata* with the second Duke of Buckingham, George Villiers, who parcelled out the York House estate and sold it in building plots for these houses, and it is noways improbable that the building scheme was placed, in whole or in part, in Wren's hands. Without attempting to state definitively therefore whose hand produced these doorways, there is at least a basis to the presumption that we have in them a relic of the genius of Wren. In themselves they are certainly pleasing, and without an undue profusion of ornament, or on the other hand, anything of the (shall we say?) forbidding character of many of the productions of the Adam brothers, they perform their function with unobtrusive grace and dignity.

To speak of Wren in work of this stamp is to imply the name of Grinling Gibbons, for Wren never lost the chance of creating a beautiful thing in wood or stone, if by placing the work with Grinling Gibbons he could secure it. So when all is said and done, it is to

H. F. Waring. del.

Fig. 2. BUCKINGHAM STREET,
ADELPHI, W. C.

Fig. 3. BUCKINGHAM STREET,
ADELPHI, W. C.

Fig. 4. GREAT ORMOND STREET,
BLOOMSBURY, W. C.

Fig. 5.   BUCKINGHAM STREET,
ADELPHI, W. C.

Fig. 6. GREAT ORMOND STREET,
BLOOMSBURY, W. C.

Fig. 7.   GREAT ORMOND STREET,
BLOOMSBURY, W. C.

Fig. 9. CHEYNE ROW, CHELSEA, S. W.

Gibbons and his followers, from Timbs onwards, that we owe all that is best in carving of the times we are discussing. These examples (Figs. 3 and 5), contemporaneous as they certainly are, go to show that even in the seventeenth century utilitarianism was but a small consideration in the design. As shelter against any but almost perpendicular rain or sun even Figure 3 would be of but slight practical service, while Figure 5 would afford practically no protection at all. At any rate, the suggestion presents itself that the occurrence of these two doorways, coeval, so differently principled, prohibits adhesion, so far as the seventeenth century is concerned, to any theory which would seek to date these features according as they differ in treatment between true weather-fences or ornaments pure and simple.

Quite as frequently as any development of this pilastered type of door head occur examples where the head is carried entirely on brackets or consoles. Of these Figure 1 furnishes a good specimen, including the effective central concavity. Though examples are obtainable which possess a greater measure of elaboration, there are not wanting in this door head (Fig. 1) signs of thoughtful and clever treatment; the proportions, as a whole, are pleasing, and there is that successful grappling with the difficulties of a combination of the arc and the right line which is not always typical of the work of the eighteenth century as a whole.

Fig. 10. GREAT COLLEGE STREET,
WESTMINSTER, S. W.

Figure 9, taken, like Figure 1, from Cheyne Row, Chelsea, S. W., is probably later; there is a note of stint in the cornice and a barrenness of spirit in the ribbed architrave that is altogether out of keeping with the elaboration of the consoles. We can imagine that, however greatly the designer may have appreciated the individual good points of designs to which he may have had access, his forte was not synthesis.

The examples shown in Figures 7 and 8 have little in common, save perhaps the degree of their elaboration of ornament. The date of Figure 7 is, in all probability, the early eighteenth century; the flat pilasters and Ionic half caps, the curiously heavy composition of the consoles, the break in the frieze and, most of all, the deep carved moulding around the doorway, all tend to place this work in that time. Figure 8 is probably a little later, say middle of the eighteenth century. Elaboration is here carried to a degree almost final; construction and Classicism are both alike sacrificed to the carver; the pilasters carry nothing and the cornice loses character.

In the example shown in Figure 11, where two doors are grouped in one design, there is room for much admiration and some speculation. In point of date the doors show much of the spirit of the time of Wren:

there is in the combination, however, a freedom from Classic form and tradition that suggests an affinity to the days of one hundred years ago. Pilasters are replaced by long shallow panels, caps are swallowed up by the consoles, small pilasters are introduced at the doorframe to support a fanlight suggestive of Chippendale, and the masks in the center of each doorway bear an aspect of modernity. Nevertheless the design is striking and, modern or not, the conception is of one to whom Wren's was a master mind.

Figure 4 represents a doorway later in date than the Adam period, but probably prior to the last example. The type is of common occurrence, and if there can be ascribed to the designer no great originality of idea, yet the spirit of the late eighteenth century is well expressed in the stricter Classicism and the more traditional proportions. A noteworthy point is the substitution of pillars for pilasters. There is not the dainty economy of the Adam period, but a stolider, less susceptible sense. In useful comparison comes Figure 2, a typical work of the Adam brothers, for the evidence is here happily complete. Classicism more severe is unlikely, yet in spite of it, perhaps because of it, we have a dignity and repose befitting the time which in a sense protested against the abandonment of Classic

Fig. 11.   QUEEN'S SQUARE, W. C.

forms to the embellisher's opportunity; it was the outcome of a craving for simplicity—product of the nausea of the general over-elaboration and license.

Figure 10 is probably not a complete composition; the consoles in fact appear so entirely foreign to the remainder of the work as to lead to the supposition that the more simple overdoor they support was not originally contemporaneous with them.

Figure 6 also is modern. Apart from the fact that the example bears date 1824, there are essential evidences of modernity. Adjoining, as it does, a number of the doorways shown in Figure 4, there is superficial reason to think that Figure 6 is contemporaneous with the rest. But, on the other hand, this very adjacency is enough to account for an eighteenth-century spirit in a nineteenth-century doorway, and there is a frank appearance of development, of having "gone one better" that leads us to regard the whole composition as late; nor, on the evidence, would 1824 appear to be a date

unsuitable to attach to the origin of this interesting doorway.

These examples, then chosen more or less at hazard, illustrate in a preliminary manner the steady swing of the pendulum from freedom to severity, from restraint to elaboration, throughout the seventeenth and eighteenth centuries, up to the nineteenth century. No doubt, given time and opportunity for research, a similar course of development would be traceable in the whole of the architecture of the periods under consideration. At any rate it may be said, without ignoring the splendid works on the history of the English Renaissance already extant, that when the history of the architectural detail of the past three centuries comes to be written, sympathetically and from an impartial point-of-view, there will be fields for analytical criticism and conjecture as wide and rich, it may be, as ever were explored by the recorders of Classic and Mediaeval architecture.

·Detail· of· ·Panel·

·Elevation·

·Detail· of· ·Carving· on· ·Jamb·

·iron·

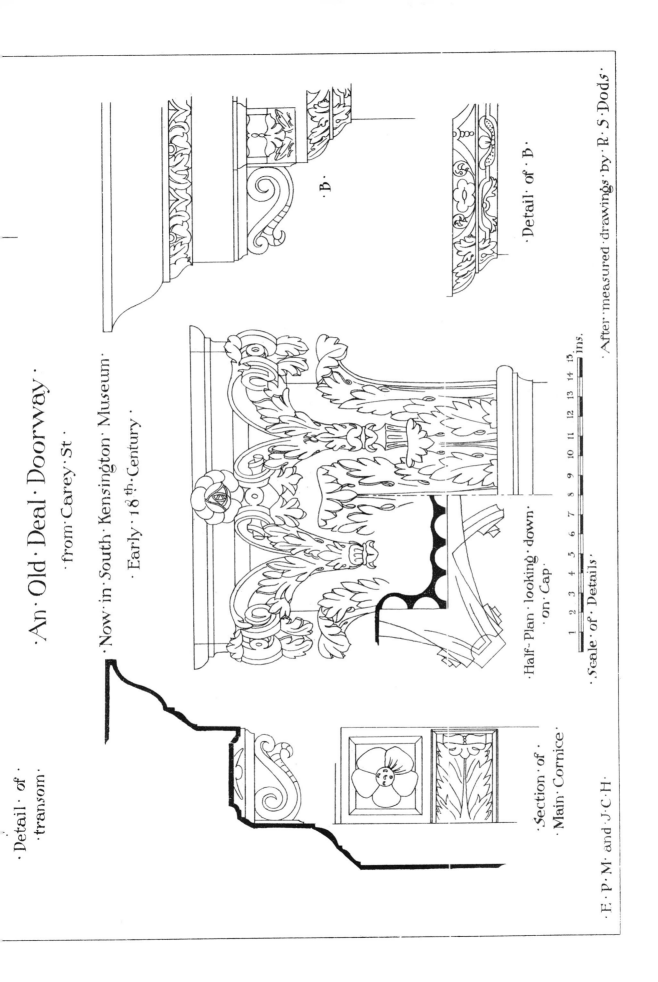

· Detail · of ·
· transom ·

· An · Old · Deal · Doorway ·

· from · Carey · St ·

· Now · in · South · Kensington · Museum ·

· Early · 18th · Century ·

· B ·

· Detail · of · B ·

· Half · Plan · looking · down ·
· on · Cap ·

1 2 3 4 5 6 7 8 9 10 11 12 13 14 15 ins.

· Scale · of · Details ·

· Section · of ·
· Main · Cornice ·

· After · measured · drawings · by · R · S · Dods ·

· F · P · M · and · J · C · H ·

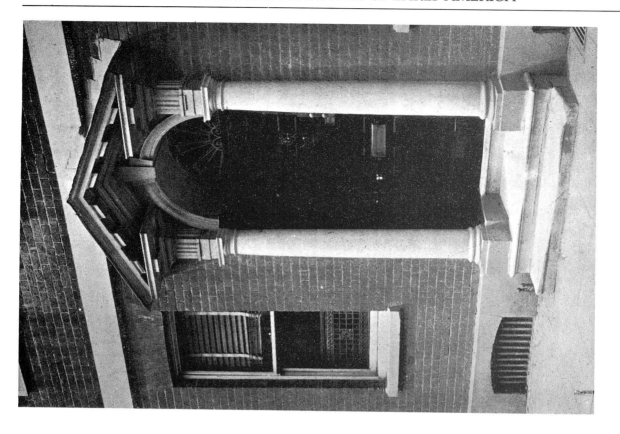

Doorway—SPITAL STREET, GUILDFORD

Doorway—E STREET, CHICHESTER

Doorway — ABINGDON

Doorway — PETWORTH, SUSSEX

· 18 th · Century · Doorheads ·

· Exeter · Eng ·

· B ·

· Width · between ·
· brackets · 3' 6" ·

· 4" thick ·

· Detail · at · B ·

· E · P · M · and · J · C · H ·

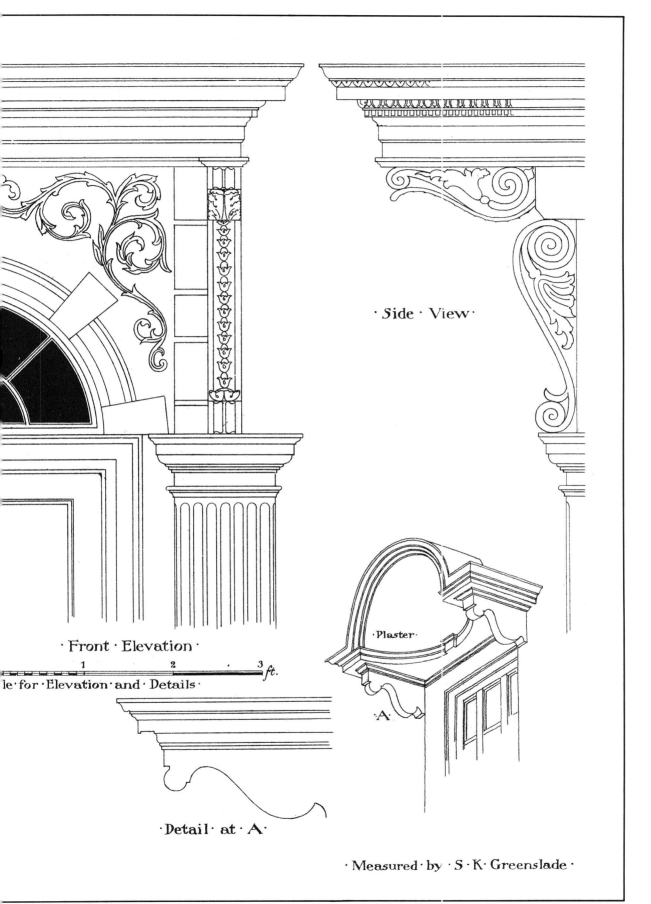

· Side · View ·

· Plaster ·

·A·

· Front · Elevation ·

1   2   3   *ft.*

le · for · Elevation · and · Details ·

· Detail · at · A·

· Measured · by · S · K· Greenslade ·

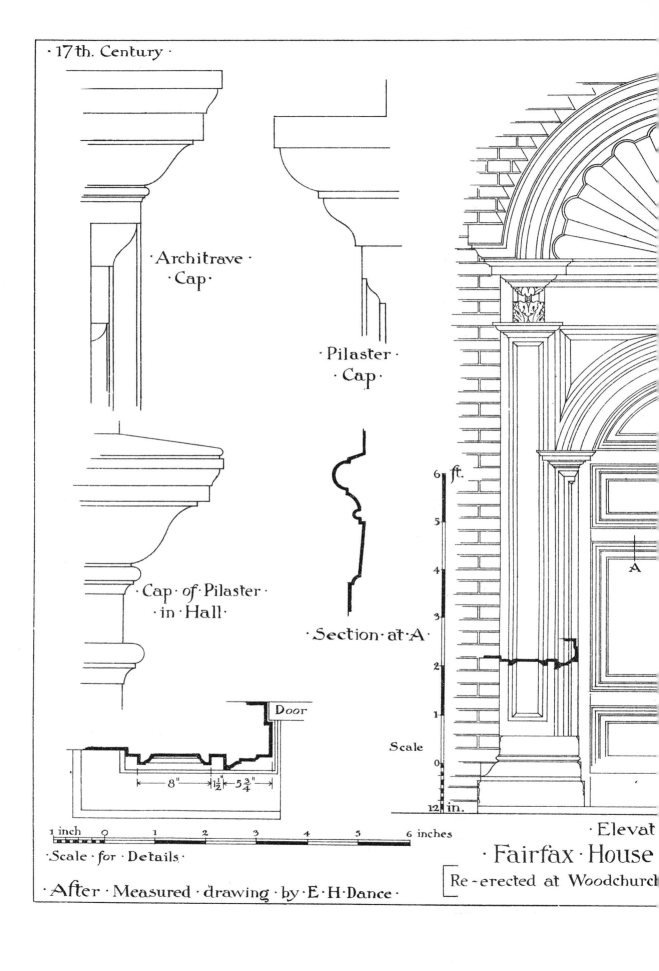

· 17th. Century ·

· Architrave ·
· Cap ·

· Pilaster ·
· Cap ·

· Cap · of · Pilaster ·
· in · Hall ·

· Section · at · A ·

Door

8"   1½"   5¾"

6 ft.

5

4

3

2

1

Scale

0

12 in.

A

· Elevat

· Fairfax · House

Re-erected at Woodchurc

1 inch   O   1   2   3   4   5   6 inches

· Scale · for · Details ·

· After · Measured · drawing · by · E · H · Dance ·

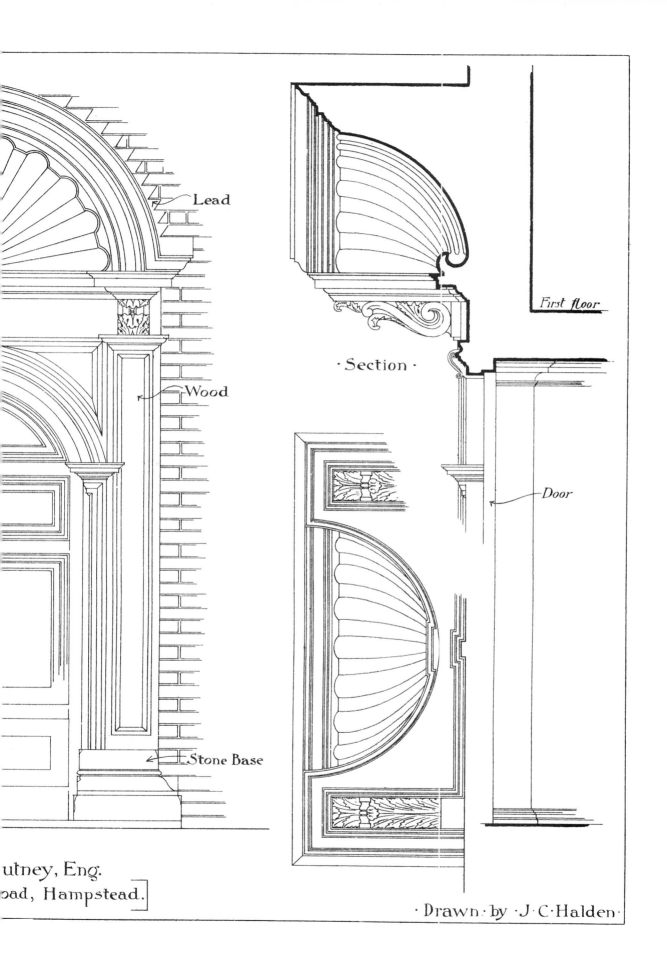

Lead

Wood

· Section ·

First *floor*

Door

Stone Base

utney, Eng.
oad, Hampstead.

·Drawn·by·J·C·Halden·

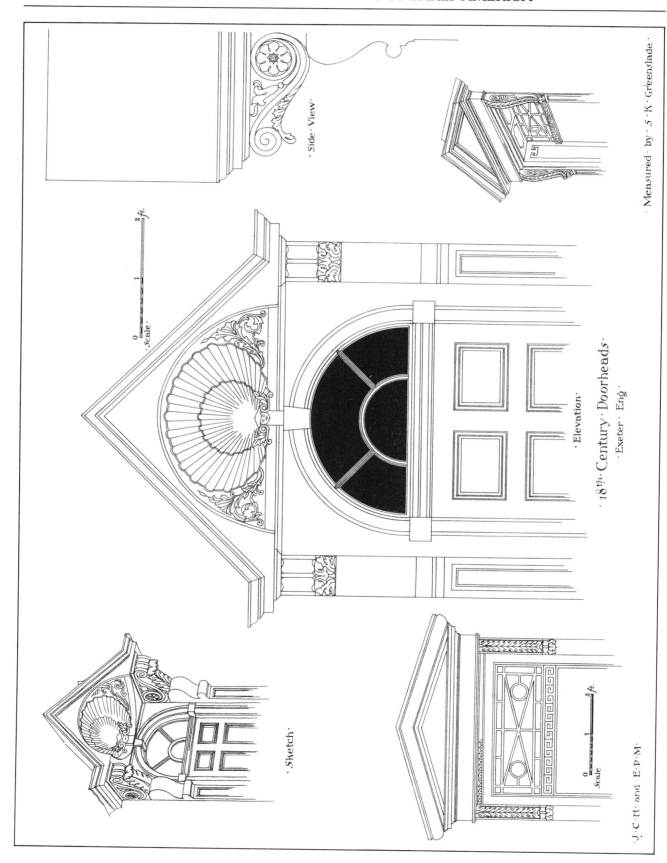

· Side · View ·

· Measured · by · S · K · Greenslade ·

· Scale ·

· Elevation ·

· 18ᵗʰ · Century · Doorheads ·
· Exeter · Eng ·

· Sketch ·

scale

·J·C·H· and ·E·P·M·

The Architecture of the Eighteenth Century in England

Text by
Paul Waterhouse
Originally published in 1900 as
Volume II of The Georgian Period

·Brentford House·
·Brentford· Middlesex·
·Eng·

THE ARCHITECTURE OF THE
EIGHTEENTH CENTURY IN ENGLAND

Architecture has its ironies, like any other field of human experience — not bitter ironies, no grim disappointments, no cruelties wrapped in mockery, but only mild, and sometimes gracious, developments of the wholly unexpected; proofs, if proof were needed, that man is no more master of his fate in architecture than in anything else. In fact, these manifestations show that architecture is a bigger force than man, its creator, and that his little will, for all its pride of power, is only, at its moments of apparent production, giving a bend here and there to the course of a resistless river. Sometimes, indeed, one learns the lesson that the greatest architect is he who helps, not hinders, the stream. The great men are not the men of novelty, still less are they the men of archaeology. A dash for originality frequently ends in the production of an unwholesome eddy; conversely, an effort at conservatism leads too often to the formation of a stagnant backwater.

Sir Christopher Wren, whom we may look upon, in a sense, as the father of English eighteenth-century architecture, was fully aware of these truths, and he at least was a man who had every excuse for viewing the case otherwise. His education, to begin with, was not architectural; his beginnings of professional life were in spheres scientific rather than artistic. He was tied by no traditions, and fettered by no scholastic or academic chains. He slipped into architecture over the wall, so to speak, like Formalist and Hypocrisy in the *Pilgrim's Progress*. And if, when he thus came into architecture from the outside, with his open mind and vigorous intellect, he had felt that the right way to go to work was to start fair, free of prejudice, free of tradition, free even of the spirit of his own age, would he not have been the very man to show the courage of

his convictions, and to embark on the adventurous career of a new architecture? Certainly he would; but what do we find? Instead of a gospel of freedom and individualism, he wrote these remarkable words: —

"It is necessary for the architect in a conspicuous work to preserve his undertaking from general censure, and so for him to accommodate his designs to the Geist of the age he lives in, though it appear to him less rational."

Strange words, which show the relation of an original mind to the force of contemporary taste. Nor can it be doubted that Wren's obedience to the commands of tradition was at least as strong as his subjection to the spirit of the age.

Now, the planting in the New World of the civilization of the Old, which took place gradually during the seventeenth and eighteenth centuries, was an opportunity such as man's history has seldom known for the establishment of a new creation in architecture. Here was a chance for the men who say that the vitality of architecture should be proved by its independence of archaeology and tradition. So long as a nation remains in its own country, and retains its accustomed civilization, so long, they might say, there is a certain excuse — if not a valid reason — for the retention of apparently meaningless traditions of form.

But here was a new state of conditions altogether. A nation — or rather a selection from various nations, full of vigorous enterprise, and therefore presumably full of the power of origination and of artistic vitality, has transferred itself to a new soil, where it is to live under new climatic environment, and even, to a certain extent, under fresh conditions of state and society. The apostles of the independence of architecture might reasonably look for a new style under these new condi-

Fig. 1. A BALUSTER SUNDIAL, SUSSEX

Northern Europe had borrowed from Italy and Italy had revived from her dead Roman self. Is this a proof of the strength of old Rome, clamoring in its grave for a share in the new territory, or is it rather a sign that man, for all his radicalism and commercialism and "modern-side" education, has in him, whether he like it or not, whether he know it or not, a latent fiber that must be fed from the ancient culture of the past? I think it is the latter.

I am far from suggesting that the architecture of the eighteenth century which flourished in the British and Dutch homes of the American immigrants is in any large degree identical with the work of Rome, or even with that of fifteenth-century Italy; indeed, if it were, it would give the lie to the undeniable law that true architecture is always affected by geographical and ethnological conditions.

The Georgian architecture—I use the word in its widest and loosest sense—is indisputably genuine architecture, a union, that is, of Beauty, Necessity and Tradition, the first-named resulting from the other two. As such it is distinguishable at a glance, like all true architecture, both from its forerunners and from its posterities. But I do hold—this is my point of argument—that its tradition of form, its symbolism and its culture are essentially and excellently Classical. Wherever, in this architecture, forms can legitimately break loose from mere construction, wherever composition stands free of mere necessitudinous building, the expression towards which it strains with all the force of well-tutored simplicity is the manifestation of the Classical. There is here no implication that architecture only reaches its development when it breaks loose from building as such—a doctrine which will sound hollow and untrue in the ears of all truth-lovers, but it is obvious that in all buildings of any generosity, in whatever style, there are points so emancipated from the exigencies of mere constructional fabric as to give special play to the exhibition of the whims, or, to speak more truly, of the spirit of their designer. Such points in a Gothic eccelesiastical building are shrines and tabernacles, sedilia and font-covers, stalls, screens and portals; in the Georgian home these playgrounds of free art are found in the cornices, chimney-pieces, porches and similar accessories. Perhaps the front door and the mantel, with some special fitness in each case, are the chief means of this expression. Rightly are they the bearers of a special message, being, as it were, the symbols, or, rather, the very instruments, respectively, of outward and inward welcome.

The examples here brought together as illustrations are a mere random handful, taken from a rich profusion scattered all over England, and meant to show how closely the things which today are loved and rev-

tions. But what is the actual result in history? Truly a wonderful event—a strange and delightful testimony to man's hold on the past, or shall we rather say, to architecture's hold upon an almost unsuspected part of human nature. The architecture of the new world was evidently to be not merely a continuance of European tradition, but, a greater marvel still, it was to echo in a kind of tertiary Renaissance the Classical culture which

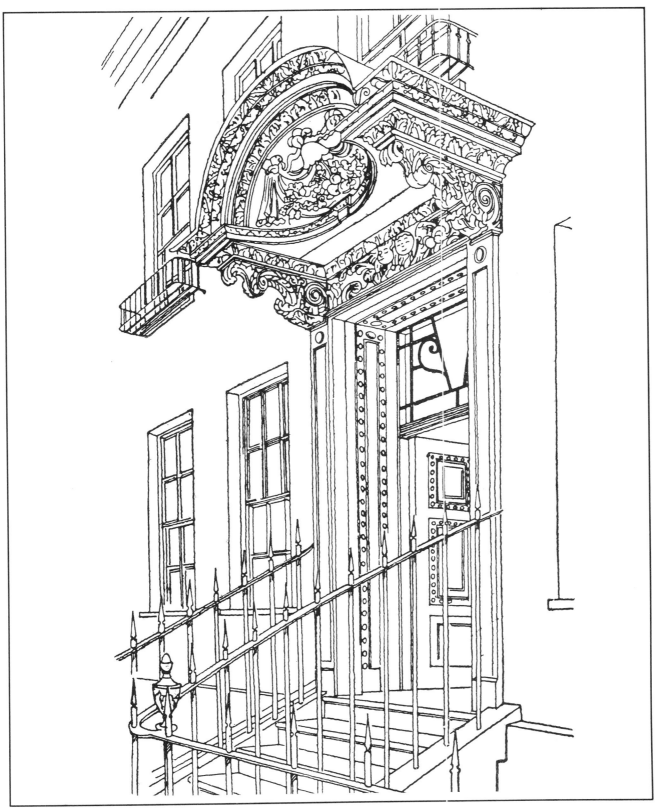

Fig. 2. NUMBER 9 GROSVENOR ROAD, LONDON

Fig. 3. *Doorway*—1722—WEST WYCOMBE, BUCKS

Fig. 4. PORCH AT ALTON, HANTS

the architectural historian, might well be held up to admiration for this, that it was a style which, in spite of its original foreign extraction, became truly vernacular. There subsisted, in those times, between architect and workman an understanding, which can hardly be said to exist at the present time. Partly, no doubt, owing to the limited range of design, and partly to the comparatively small field of antiquity open to the pursuit of the designer, it became possible for workmen of intelligence in various trades—but especially in those of the joiner and mason—to have at their fingers' ends a knowledge, and an accurate knowledge, of the mouldings and features of which their architects were making use. Nay, more, it is the result of this intimate knowledge on the part of the workman that the humbler buildings of the town and the village (which were often, no doubt, in those days, as in our own, constructed without the intervention of an architectural designer at all) have about them that undeniable stamp of correctness of design which, whether you are pleased to call it archaeological or not, results in something uncommonly like a display of good taste.

The architecture of the period was not, I was beginning to say, entirely of this minor domestic type. Side by side with the simpler house-buildings the century witnessed the development of a greater Classical style, which, but for certain lapses, one might call Palladian,

erenced in the United States are allied to those beauties of architecture which we cherish as having been enjoyed in this country one hundred and two hundred years ago. To be sure, they are vanishing, perhaps more rapidly with us than they are with you, but they linger yet, even in certain quiet streets of London, into which one steps as into an atmosphere of antiquity more insistent in its way than that which pervades the great cathedrals. One feels of a Westminster Abbey that it is in a sense no more old than it is new—it is of all time. A great church built of enduring stone has about it a quality of everlastingness, which likens it to the earth and sky, of whose antiquity there is no more consciousness than doubt. But when, out of some crowded thoroughfare of modern buildings, one branches into a street lined with the comparatively frail homes of five or six generations ago, one feels an overwhelming sense of the presence of one's forefathers. The very fragility of these slender pilasters and delicate mouldings adds to the marvel of their continuity. Their survival is like the survival of a man. Besides, there is in human nature a kind of contrariety which does not honor antiquity in the direct ratio of years. The Pantheon, even from the point of age, possesses a greater charm than the Pyramids.

But I must not write of our eighteenth century as if its architectural work were all of the minor domestic type. Undoubtedly there is a great architectural importance in the simpler domestic work of the period, which, if it had no other claim upon the attention of

Fig. 5. *Door Head*—HASTINGS

Fig. 6. *Chimneypiece*—HIGH WYCOMBE, BUCKS

and which might be looked upon as a direct outcome of Wren's accustomed manner, which in turn may be termed a consequence of Inigo Jones. In this work, too, in the monumental and palace architecture as well as in the domestic, the study and proficiency of the individual workman was a large factor in the success of the art. This point has been well brought out in Mr. Reginald Blomfield's excellent work on the Renaissance in England, which affords the best available summary of the architectural facts of the century we are discussing. One might be tempted to say that this period of architecture had two sides—on the one hand the correctness of Wren, and on the other a Dutch importation which gave character to the humbler street architecture. But we find that Wren himself, after the accession of William and Mary and the consequent introduction of Dutch taste, was among the first

to borrow his architecture from Holland, and may thus be said to be himself the father of both aspects of eighteenth-century British architecture. The names of architects associated with the early Restoration are not conspicuous, but we might mention among them such workers as Bell, of King's Lynn, who executed various works in his own neighborhood, including the well-known customhouse in his own town, and a picturesque church at North Runcton, dated 1713, that may be looked upon as a type of those Georgian churches (sometimes rather quaint than beautiful) which the architects of the Gothic Revival did their best to sweep from the land. The great names which succeeded Wren's are, of course, Vanbrugh and Hawksmoor, whose works I imagine have but little parallel in the architecture of America. Vanbrugh's palaces—though his reputation has suffered from too general an appli-

Fig. 7. *Chimneypiece*—HALTON HOUSE,
HASTINGS, SUSSEX

cation of his well-known epitaph—must be acknowledged to be heavy buildings. The less-known example here given (Fig. 16) is lighter in character than the more celebrated Blenheim and Castle Howard. Hawksmoor's genius is in many ways more attractive, and certainly more inventive. His church in Spitalfields—the spire of which is of a most unusual type—can certainly not be objected to on grounds of dull formality, nor can the familiar front of St. Mary's Woolnoth, near the Mansion House, which so nearly suffered destruction a few years ago in the interests of railway traffic.

Of all the stars that had power to make their light seen in the wake of Wren there is, perhaps, none brighter than James Gibbs. It was his cultivated genius that made itself known in the Church of St. Martin, in Trafalgar Square, in the beautiful St. Mary-le-Strand, which blocks with a gracious interference the busy crowd in one of London's densest thoroughfares, and also in the Radcliffe Library (Fig. 19)—a circular building of wholly unusual design which occupies a quiet square in the collegiate city of Oxford. Gibbs had other opportunities of conspicuous work, notably the Senate House at Cambridge, but none of his buildings exceed in beauty and in classic refinement the two London churches or the Oxford Library. I have no wish to take the reader through a list of English eighteenth-century architects—some of the best-known names come indeed at the close of the century, and, therefore, belong to a period which cannot be said to have any true affinity with the American Colonial work—but there are still two names among the producers of what I have styled monumental architecture which deserve a passing mention, the names of Dean Aldrich,

Fig. 8. OFFICES IN HIGH STREET, LEWES, SUSSEX

of Oxford, and of John Wood, of Bath. The former is a brilliant example of the architectural amateur. Holding the Deanery of Christ Church, which implies not so much an ecclesiastical appointment as the mastership of the College of that name, Aldrich may be supposed to have had occupations enough to leave little time for artistic hobbies. But he was a man of unusual versatility—not only was he a good classic scholar, he was also a logician, and wrote a treatise on logic which remained for many generations of students the standard textbook. He was no inconsiderable musician: there is at least one psalm-chant and more than one anthem due to his skill as a composer, and with all these many fields of energy he still found time to handle architecture also, both from a theoretical and practical standpoint. His *Elements of Architecture* written in imitation of Vitruvius, and written in Latin, too, is, to be sure, pretty nearly forgotten—being rather elegant than useful; but his buildings, chief of which is the Church of All Saints in High Street, remain as enduring memorials of his academic power in an art which but few amateurs have successfully invaded. It is not known to what extent Dean Aldrich had professional aid in the working out of his designs, but no architect's name has ever been connected with them and no tradition has ever assailed his claim to at least the leading share in the buildings with which his name is associated. I am glad to remind Americans of Dean Aldrich's claims.

John Wood was an artist before whom exceptional opportunities were spread. It is not at all clear where he learned his architecture, and he appears to have started life as a road-surveyor in 1727. But he found himself in Bath at the time when Bath was waking up to the possibility of getting itself rebuilt, and under the patronage of Ralph Allen, an enterprising owner

of property, and, which is more important, an owner of quarries, he was enabled to put an entirely new aspect upon an old town. The most conspicuous of his works was Prior Park, a magnificent residence, with a hexastyle Corinthian portico, outside the town; but his genius was more exhaustively taxed in the schemes for laying-out streets and squares in the city itself. In this work Wood (who was practically the pioneer in England of combined composition in street architecture) exhibited the most fertile ingenuity. His squares, his terraces, his crescents and his circular colonnades are masterpieces in their way and evince a brilliant talent in the exceptional art of architecture on a comprehensive scale.

But it is time to leave the consideration of the monumental art of the century and to look to those similar buildings which in their, often nameless, obscurity may really be said to form the backbone of English eighteenth-century architecture. In passing on to them, let me merely mention two examples of which illustrations are here given. One is the colonnade, or entrance screen, at Syon House on the Thames, and the other the Church of All Saints at Northampton. The colonnade is, strictly speaking, too late for our period, belonging, as I suppose, to the time, if not to the actual handiwork, of the Brothers Adam, but it is so elegant an example of the century's idea of domestic magnificence and, for that matter, so good a piece of art, that I have no mind to leave it out of this collection. The Northampton Church, on the other hand, is, I think, Stuart rather than Georgian, but it is a rich and characteristic specimen of the way in which the architects of the English Renaissance laid Classic hands on the hitherto Gothic domain of the church. I wish in

Fig. 9. THE VICARAGE, LEWISHAM

Fig. 10. HOUSE—1731—GUILDFORD

Fig. 11. A HOUSE IN THE CLOSE, SALISBURY

this connection that I had an illustration to offer of the small and interesting church of Little Stanmore, near Edgware. It has an ancient Gothic tower, but the entire nave and chancel, within and without, are of the strictest Georgian Classic. Tradition, perhaps falsely, connects the church and its organ with Handel, and the churchyard contains the grave of the supposed impersonation of Handel's "Harmonious Blacksmith;" but be the tradition true or false, the church in its design is a near counterpart in architecture of that academic spirit which prevails in Handelian church music.

Midway between the monumental buildings of the eighteenth century (the churches and mansions) and the humbler domestic architecture stand the town halls of small market centers and the multitudinous almshouses. The town halls are very characteristic and often very beautiful examples of the century's work.

Among the best of them is that at Abingdon, near Oxford an out-of-the-way building which is sometimes ascribed to no less an author than Vanbrugh. It is extremely graceful, and its air of rather excessive correctness and propriety gives it just that seal of distinction which should differentiate the home of the *community* from the homes of its component *individuals*. Its correctness is tempered, oddly enough, by a very unusual departure from Classic rule. On each of its sides the center is occupied by a "solid," not by a "void"—whereas the laws of composition call for an arch in the center—never a pier. The Council Chamber at Chichester has the same air of solemnity without the same grace. It seems hardly able to accomplish its own Palladian intentions, and the gruesome lion which surmounts its top gives a bathos to the composition which one would not expect. The century is by no means weak in carving, least of all in heraldic carving;

Fig. 12. SCHOOLHOUSE, CRANBROOK, KENT

the stone unicorn from the Carlisle Parade, Hastings, and the two examples of Royal Arms from Cranbrook and South Moulton are quite enough to prove that the sculptors of the Georgian period were real masters of a conventional school of animal carving which has seldom been surpassed. The same excellent power is displayed in the cartouche from the South Moulton town hall, doubtless an effort by the same hand that carved the Royal Arms. The town hall itself is a good specimen of its kind—a typical façade with a main story of Corinthian pilasters standing on a basement formed of the inevitable town hall arcade. The pilasters and their entablature are surmounted by a good pediment, and above the roof is an attractive clock-turret with a weather-cock. The Rye town hall is an example of a rather simpler treatment, and so is the well-proportioned building at Witney. That at High Wycombe, if simple in its upper story, is more ambitious in its arcade, which shows a clever arrangement in the grouping of the columns, whereby the additional stability required at the angles is obtained without solid piers. The roof-lantern here is especially graceful, and I am glad to be able to give a photograph of it in detail (Fig. 20). The town halls here exemplified are but a few examples out of a great profusion of such buildings that are to be found in county towns all over the country. Not less numerous and not less interesting are the almshouses, of which in some towns several examples are to be found. Salisbury, for instance, has three or four, and many other places can show two or more. The College of Matrons, just within the precincts of the Cathedral-close at Salisbury is, at least outwardly, a building typical of its class—so also, in a less ambitious vein, is the Banks Almshouse, at Maidstone (Fig. 21), which dates from 1700. The little lantern (Fig. 18), bearing date 1707, is from a similar building—Christ's Hospital—at Abingdon, and the court yard view of the Tomkins Almshouses (Fig. 22) shows a rather later building in the same town.

The coaching inns of the towns on the old highroads

Fig. 13. NEWBY HALL—1720—YORKS
By Campbell

are often of very good architecture, but few of them are so ambitious as the well-known White Hart at Salisbury.

I am fortunately able, owing to the industry of Mr. Galsworthy Davie, whose wandering camera seems never to let a good thing pass, to give many examples of ordinary street domestic and shop architecture. It would, I think, be undesirable and unprofitable for me to attempt to allude in writing to each of these illustrations. They tell for themselves their own tale of quiet beauty, and bear an eloquent testimony to the age of culture gentility which they represent. We may have surpassed our forefathers in some qualities of mind and intellect, but there is, to take a single example, a spirit of gentlemanly confidence about the really handsome Lewes shop-front (Fig. 8) which, to my mind, entices customers quite as readily as plate-glass and stanchions can do. The bay window at Rye (Fig. 23) is to me a particularly fascinating product of the art of the period. It is not a house window, but the window of a garden room. You would enter this rural parlor, no doubt, from a green lawn in a walled orchard—and making your way to the window-seat would find yourself looking out onto the bustling little street. It is this happy combination of business and seclusion, of town and country, of garden life and street life, which is the key to the amenity of Georgian existence. Folk realized in those days that it was alike a great convenience to live in a street, and a great hardship to live without a garden—with the result that their front doors were placed on the pavement and their back doors were practically in the country. The town of Lewes is laid out entirely on this principle, and the result is that it consists mainly of two parallel streets with a tract of green country between them. Nowadays the increased value of land renders such an arrangement unduly costly, and we have had to face as a result the growth of suburbs. It was practically only

in London that the suburb took its rise as early as the middle of last century, and it is fair to own that when the value of land began to produce this result in our crowded capital it did not produce it in its modern form. The villages around London which became the rural homes of London merchants knew little of our modern rage for purchasing a plot, planting a house at the back of it, and devoting the rest of the site to a serpentine carriage drive. The man of the eighteenth century, in his suburb as in his town, was content to put his door on the street and to use the whole of his unoccupied land as secluded garden.

I had hoped to be able to offer a photograph of a typical English street of the eighteenth century. I should probably have taken my example from Blandford, a little Dorsetshire town which had the misfortune to be entirely destroyed by fire about the year 1740, with the fortunate result that, having been entirely rebuilt at that date, most of its houses have managed to survive to the present day, thus presenting a homogeneous collection of Georgian town architecture. I have, as it happens, failed in this attempt, but I am able to show instead a view of Northbrook Street, Newbury (Fig. 34), which, though marred by some modern interpolations, gives something of the effect of one of these old-world thoroughfares. Newbury further provides a good example of an eighteenth-century bridge. Great pains and no little art were expended on bridges during this period. They were recognized as occasions for a certain amount of architectural display, and the necessity for stout stone-constructions together with the need of a balustrade has generally led to their having a certain Palladian character. The Chester Bridge, familiar to many a newly landed American tourist, which carries the high-level wall walk across one of the main entrances to the town, is a good instance of Georgian design in this class of work.

The age was not one of great ecclesiastical fervor, the rebuilding of the London City churches being a result rather of the accident of the Great Fire than of any ecclesiological spirit, and we must not, therefore, look for much display of art in church fittings, but there are certain notable exceptions. In metalwork, some of which was ecclesiastical, the century is very strong. The two chandeliers, Dutch in character, here illustrated (Figs. 29, 30) are as good as they need be and are worthy of the excellent standard which prevailed in smiths' work generally. All kinds of grilles (Fig. 35), whether as chancel-screens or entrance-gates, were carried out during this period with noticeable skill, and Wren himself was in this, as in other departments of his art, the father and forerunner of his successors. Pulpits and stalls were sometimes moderately well executed. Not many altars date from the century,

Fig. 14. HOUSE AT BRENTFORD, MIDDLESEX

Fig. 15. HOUSE AT ALTON, HANTS

Fig. 16. OULTON HALL, CHESHIRE
Sir John Vanbrugh, Architect

but there is a good one at Rye, if somewhat unusual in its design. It will be seen that the frontal, baffled by the disregard of precedent displayed by the table, has solved its difficulty by getting inside (Fig. 32)!

Finally and fittingly let me end these examples with the tombs. We have seen the Georgian man in his home — be it a palace in a park or a house in a street; we have noted the warm welcome of his court and of his hearth; we have looked at his church and at his council chamber; we have seen the inn that welcomed his prosperity, the almshouse that sheltered his adversity; we have passed in review his colleges and his schools. Let us now, for an ending, follow him to his grave. Even there he lies beneath the touch of that old humanity which graced the accessories of his life. A Classic baluster (Fig. 1) bore the gnomon on which the sun marked his fleeting days, a Classic console decks the angles of his tomb and a Classic cornice rims its heavy lid. And if, as well might be, his virtues and the grief of his posterity called for some record within the church's walls that should outlast the weather-beaten panels of the sepulcher outside, there was placed in aisle or nave same graceful composition of Ionic or Corinthian forms (Fig. 36) which framed a story of his living and dying, written as often as not in the very tongue of ancient Rome.

[Through unfamiliarity with the physical requirements of bookmaking, Mr. Waterhouse, in his modesty, has cut his paper short before providing matter enough to "carry" the illustrations that accompany it, no one of which can be spared, and obviously long before he had said everything about his subject he would like to say and which we and his readers can only regret that he has not said. It is, however, a mat-

ter of gratulation that we are able to satisfy the printer's requirements by appending to the foregoing paper parts of an article written upon a cognate subject by Mr. Waterhouse and published in the *Architectural Review* (London) a year or two ago (c1900). — WARE]

"The Palladian dictum that the door is to be proportioned to the magnificence of the owner is one that has found general modern acceptance, though perhaps not exactly in the original sense. A door being primarily an entrance for men, there underlies our thought of every door the consideration that its size has been regulated by the human standard. You see a door six feet high in a cottage and one eight feet high in a villa, and you conclude from the contrast that the one is inhabited by a being of normal size who will stoop if need be, but that the other is the abode of a stiff-necked and high-headed creature who adds to his own height by a silk hat, and to his wife's by heels and feathers. This is the rudimentary application of the Palladian theory removed only one stage from the wigwam phase of civilization when, maybe, the chief had room to go into his hut on his knees, while his subjects crawled in like the serpent upon their — watch-pockets. But the Palladian theory goes farther, and takes account not merely of modern devices for adding a fraction of a cubit to man's stature, but also of those less measurable attributes, such as worth and wealth, which differentiate human beings more surely than feet lineal. . . .

"I suppose that the humanity of doorways has never been better emphasized than in the English architecture of the last century. The early days of the English Renaissance showed, as regards external architecture,

Fig. 17. HAMPTON COURT PALACE
Sir Christopher Wren, Architect

no excess of modesty. We may without calumny brand the sixteenth-century elevations as meretricious. With the next age came chastity. Inigo Jones and his Palladianism bore the mark of comely propriety. The next age, the age of Anne, was prim, if you like, and eminently modest — but it was reserved for the reign of the brothers Adam and their contemporaries to reduce elevation (or exalt it) to prudery. They at least were no Pharisees. We can level against them no taunt of whitened sepulcher nor suggestion of inward uncleanness of cup and platter. Within all was fair and rich, delicate and elaborate — but without — what? Sometimes the grandeur, recognizable, if restrained, of Fitzroy Square and Portland Place, but more often the prudent monotony of Harley Street.

"I will not stay here to discuss whether it is altogether ignoble to consider that architecture *may* be composed of stock bricks and rectangular holes. I am not sure but that there is a nobility of asceticism here which stands on a high level; with this, however, I will not make our concern. I am only anxious now to give attention to the fact that the men of this school — not merely the 'Brothers' personally, but their contemporaries and neighbors in time — who recognized the possibility, nay the propriety of composition by sheer undecorated fenestration, were not the men to forget the door and its humanity. In the bleakest specimen of 'brick and hole' architecture, if it be of the good period, there is at least some recognition — often a very hearty recognition — of the admirable theory, or tradition, that the front door is, so to speak, a bit of the inside whose duty it is to come to the front with a welcome to the passer-by, and to show without some touch of the hospitality within.

"The mere function of giving shelter between bell-ringing and door opening provides an initial excuse for geniality. The very houses where bells are absent and even knockers, and where the door-opener has only to step across the floor of one room before the visitor is let in, profess the same amenity. Shelter, or pretended shelter, is often afforded as the one external luxury of the house. . . .

"In houses of more pretension, a favorite device in all parts of England is the well-known and graceful shell. The examples here given illustrate this familiar friend beyond need of description. A bracket on either side, springing either from a pilaster or from a less ambitious jamb, supports the angles of the shelter, the mouldings of which between the supports recede in a semi-circular form. Upon the basis of the curved plan thus formed is erected — if one may apply such a term to vacuity — a hollow, which takes approximately the shape of a quarter sphere. When it is added that the brackets carry all the foliage they can, that the framework of the whole is composed of the formal delicacies of a Roman cornice, and that the hollow is imprinted with the convolutions of a conventional shell, all has been said by way of description that can be said, except by drawing. But there is an inner sentiment in the thing that cannot be passed over, any more than it can be drawn or described. In itself it is a cardinal proof that your Englishman is, or at one time was, no utilitarian. The 'shell porch' is as arrant a piece of useless beauty as you may lay your finger on in a long search. Its logical origin, to be sure, is the board and bracket which, in simpler doorways, keeps the rain off the waiting visitor. To this simple expedient art has, bit by bit, added the luxuries of beauty, twisting and turning first one feature and then another, until, as result, a composition was produced whose fair and fascinating

Fig. 18. *Lantern* — CHRIST'S HOSPITAL, ABINGDON

outline merited adoption and repetition. But in the march of beauty, how far has the claim of function been forgotten! Ours is a country neither equatorial nor windless, so that neither sun nor rain are vertical in their attacks. It comes to pass, therefore, that the man at the door, unless he chooses carefully his hour and his day, will get neither shade nor shelter from the fair white woodwork which sits like a smile on the face of his friend's abode. Thank Heaven there are better things in this life than commodity and common sense, and thank Heaven, too, for the 'shell porch,' which is evidence in point. . . .

"This is no historical account of doors and doorways, nor even a logical one, else I would accuse myself of violated precedence in plunging thus early into the advanced glory of the shell. I should have spoken earlier of what one may call 'entablature doorways' in general. I say entablature doorways, not columnar doorways, because there are many examples that enjoy the entablature without columns, and in the majority of cases where a columnar treatment is used pilasters are substituted for the round pillars of stricter architecture. . . .

"The door of the Brentford house, which boasts what one may call the Adamite version of the Greek Corinthian, is obviously more decorous. The modillions to be sure are missed, but their absence is more than made up for by the brilliant chastity of the whole

Fig. 19. RADCLIFFE LIBRARY
James Gibbs, Architect

Cupola
Fig. 20. TOWN HALL, HIGH WYCOMBE, BUCKS

Fig. 21. BANKS ALMSHOUSE — 1700 — FAITH
STREET, MAIDSTONE

composition. There is one fault, small but awful, which a layman's eye would perhaps pass over — the slight excess in the diameter immediately above the necking of the capitals. This is no doubt a crime rather of execution than of design, but it is a lamentable defect in a work of art whose niceties are as delicate as the beauty of a face. . . .

"From examples of this sort, where the columns stand free, it is but a step to a simpler and less functional, but scarcely less beautiful, type, in which the columns are attached to the face of the wall. Here, as in an example from Dorking, utility gives way wholly to ornament. There is no pretense of shelter; the entire composition, columns and entablature, has become frankly a framework, and nothing more. Were I called to choose between these two, I would be honest, give up the choice, and clamor for compromise.

"The next stage in the development (if I may continue this process of evolution, which is possibly logical, but not necessarily historical) is the reduction of the attached columns to mere pilasters. I confess a

preference for other types, but this is no implication that I deny the beauty of this one.

"Of the doorways that altogether discard the column, even in its pilaster form, there is no lack of examples. Their habit is to carry a more or less projecting cornice on a corbel or console. Sometimes these corbels take their bed on a plain face adjoining the doorframe, sometimes upon the frame itself — sometimes upon a sort of parody of a pilaster. There are cases in which cherubs form a part either of the supporting members or of the decoration, being, no doubt, a Protestant version of the blessing which the Roman Church invokes in the words '*Inter parietes domus istius angeli Tui lucis inhabitent.*' . . .

"I will now go back to a rich example at Groombridge Place — rich, not in the overlaying of decoration, but in the multiplicity of simple parts. It is, in fact, not a porch but a colonnade, or, rather, it is a mixture of both. Architects will at once notice a remarkable feature in the composition. The entablature is level, while the balustrade rakes with the steps, and

Fig. 22. TOMKINS
ALMSHOUSE — 1733 — ABINGDON

Fig. 23. *Bay Window*—RYE, SUSSEX

Fig. 24. *Bay Window* — SAINT CROSS, NEAR WINCHESTER

yet two of the columns are based at the lower and six at the higher level. How are the proportions manoeuvred? Briefly, by a disregard of the orthodox dimensions which, oddly enough, is in this case acceptable. The taller columns are over ten diameters high — the smaller just nine. It is possible that the effect from the outside, where the difference is abetted by the diminution of perspective, is better than the appearance from within, where the two would run counter. I cannot say, for I know it only from photographs.

"But we have been dealing in details, and have lost sight of the door-humanity. Where, you will ask, does the humanity come in in the examples before us? That is more than I can tell anyone who doesn't feel it for himself; but I can suggest a point-of-view from which it will become visible to most people. Do you notice that the houses on which these doorways grow are very largely buildings of extreme simplicity? They have perhaps a bit of extravagance about their eaves-cornices, but their walls are mostly plain brick, and their windows plain openings formed in the simplest fashion of which their material admits. But what of the doorway? It could have been a plain opening, too — a severe oblong, with a square brick arch atop and plain brick sides, filled with the simplest possible framing of wood that would keep out thieves and weather. Had it been so it would in many of the examples have only been in keeping constructionally with the ascetic character of the rest of the work. But what do we find instead? — elaboration, expense, excess, *affectation* (if you dare to use the word when you should say, rather, studied grace), and sometimes frivolity. These qualities, what are they but human? What you find in these doors is no rule-of-thumb from the polytechnics, no mere offspring of builder's craft and borough by-laws, but a bit of pure human effusion. Let us go farther and strain a point, for what good is there in points if you can't strain them? You know what 'humanity' meant among the Quattrocentists. Today, at Oxford, we keep that meaning alive in giving the name of *literae humaniores* to the whole wealth of Classic literature and the histories and philosophies which it contains. It has been well said that the two great discoveries of the Renaissance were the discovery of the world and the discovery of man. And the man whom the men of that day found was no new man, but the old Adam of Greece and Rome. Humanity with them was Classicism; the humanists indeed were students of man, but the man-nature they studied was the man of their own dead Italy and the man of Hellas. Now for our stretched point, if, indeed, it can be said to be stretched: the door of these last-century houses is certainly *human* in the sense that it, most of all features of the house, breathes a spirit of Classic tradition. We live among miracles, and so rub shoulders with the marvellous that we deny the wonder of half the portents which lie under our noses; but of all the astonishing things that a traveler hurries past as he finds his way through remote country villages and little sleepy market-towns, there is to my mind nothing so amazingly incredible as the ubiquitous witness of that fantastic and lovable revival which took place between the shores of the Adriatic and the Mediterranean, four hundred years ago. And in all this multitude of testimony there is nothing that bears its part so bravely and so consistently as the front door of a solid, stolid insular Briton's house. Here, if anywhere on the face of a home, however simple, is found the opportunity for Latinism — or, if you will, for humanism; and thus it comes about by a chain of circumstances too strong to

Fig. 25. SHOP FRONT, HIGH STREET,
LEWES, SUSSEX

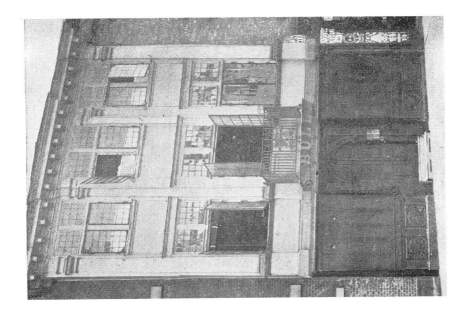

Fig. 26. BULL INN, GUILDFORD

Fig. 27. BAY WINDOW, HIGH STREET, GUILDFORD

Fig. 28. HOUSE—1700—BATTLE, SUSSEX

be resisted and almost too marvellous to be believed, that here a farmer, there a country doctor, now a publican, and now a grocer cherishes upon the countenance of his simple abode (or possibly only tolerates, but still maintains) the faithful echo of a great Italian culture which in itself was the echo of the art of two great dead nations. How appropriately the butcher, the baker, and the candlestickmaker of many an unlearned hamlet might stand in his porch in all a Briton's pride and say for himself, in more senses than he will ever understand (and in a language whose very survival is a proof of my contention) that world-known saying, which an old suburban tossed across the garden-wall in one of Terence's plays, *'Homo sum humani nihil a me alienum puto,'* which being interpreted, in a free kind of way, runs, 'I am a man, what more do you want by way of excuse for my pilasters and entablature. My good sir, they are but humanities.'

"Some may think that the door-designers who have been content to cling so closely to a limited range of types give evidence of a deficient fancy, and therefore of a deficient art. We know that identification of the power to design with a capacity for novelty and change. It is the very proof that the secrets of art are not the property of the multitude. The patient iteration of acknowledged beauty, the faithful continuance of tradition, the humility which seeks rather the production of excellence than the notoriety of novelty—all these are badges, not of mediocrity but of that gracious continence which is the very mother of good art."

Fig. 29. *Candelabrum*—CHURCH OF ST. MARY,
HORSMONDEN, KENT

Fig. 30. *Candelabrum* — NORTHIAM, SUSSEX

Fig. 32 *Altar-table*—NORTH CHAPEL

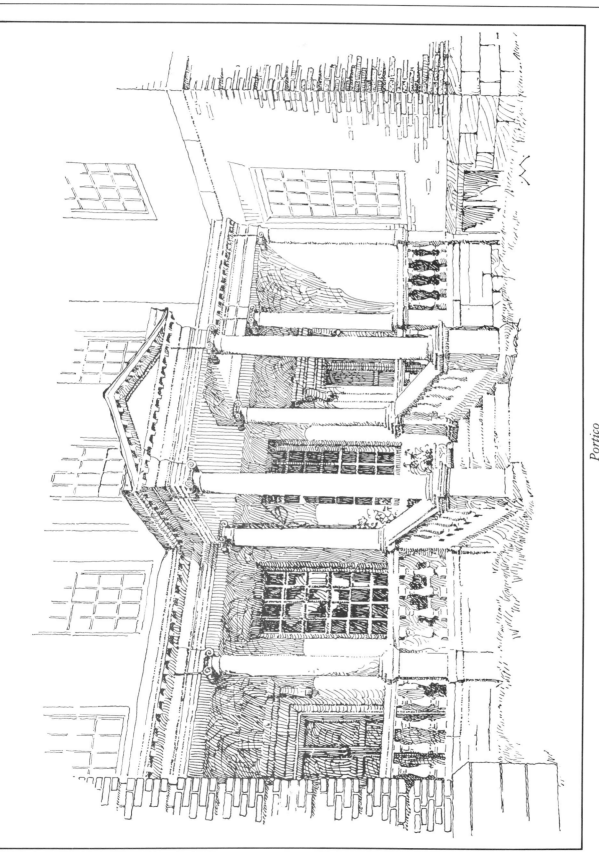

Portico
**Fig. 33. GROOMBRIDGE PLACE, NEAR
TUNBRIDGE-WELLS, ENGLAND**

Fig. 34. NORTHBROOK STREET, NEWBURY, BERKS[1]

[1] By permission of Mr. T. Hawkins.

Fig. 35. *Iron Gate* — THE TEMPLE, LONDON

Memorial Tablet
Fig. 36. ATHERINGTON CHURCH,
NORTH DEVON, ENGLAND

CHIPPENDALE'S SHOP

Admirers of Chippendale furniture may be interested to know that the curiously carved stone doorway left temporarily standing at 60 St. Martin's Lane, Charing Cross (the adjoining property having been demolished) was once the entrance to Chippendale's workshops and timber-yard. Chippendale's great rival, Cobb, had workshops not far away, at the corner of St. Martin's Lane and what is now Garrick Street.

WREN'S LONDON HOUSE

The dwelling of Sir Christopher Wren is now a national school in Botolph Lane, London. The house still contains a finely carved wooden staircase, but his private chapel has become a warehouse, with a window over the ceiling. Near by stands the church said to have been designed by his daughter, and which is peculiar in that the stone of which it is built remains white to some extent in spite of all the city smoke.

Cartouche
TOWN HALL, SOUTH MOULTON, DEVON

Royal Arms
TOWN HALL, SOUTH MOULTON, DEVON

Royal Arms
ST. DUNSTAN'S CHURCH, CRANBROOK, KENT

Pier Termination
CARLISLE PARADE, HASTINGS, SUSSEX

TOWN HALL, SOUTH WATTON, DEVON, ENGLAND

TOWN HALL, RYE, SUSSEX, ENGLAND

TOWN HALL, ABINGDON, BERKS, ENGLAND

TOWN HALL, WITNEY, OXON, ENGLAND

TOWN HALL, HIGH WYCOMBE, BUCKS, ENGLAND

THE VICARAGE, HAILSHAM, SUSSEX, ENGLAND

A HOUSE IN THE CLOSE, SALISBURY, ENGLAND

The house was destroyed in 1718.

BENHAM — 1775 — BERKS, ENGLAND

Photograph by T. W. Righton

COLLEGE OF MATRONS, IN THE CLOSE, SALISBURY, ENGLAND

THE BRIDGE, NEWBURY, BERKS, ENGLAND

Photograph by Hawkins

THE BRIDGE, NEWBURY, BERKS, ENGLAND

Entrance Screen
SYON HOUSE, MIDDLESEX, ENGLAND

ALL SAINTS' CHURCH, NORTHAMPTON, ENGLAND

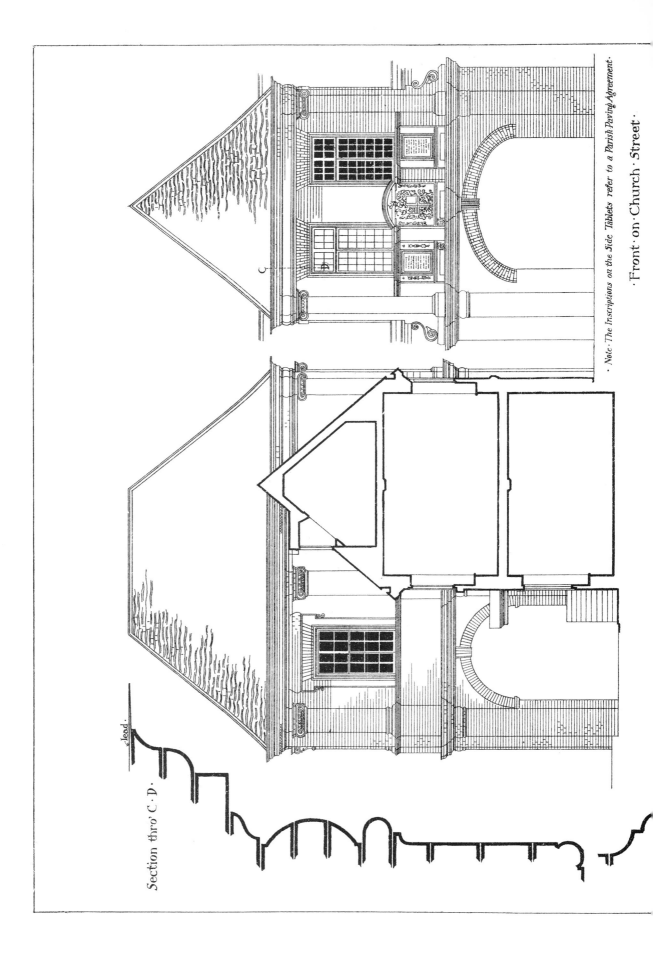

Section thro' C·D·

·lead·

·Front·on·Church·Street·

· Note· The Inscriptions on the Side Tablets refer to a Parish Paving Agreement·

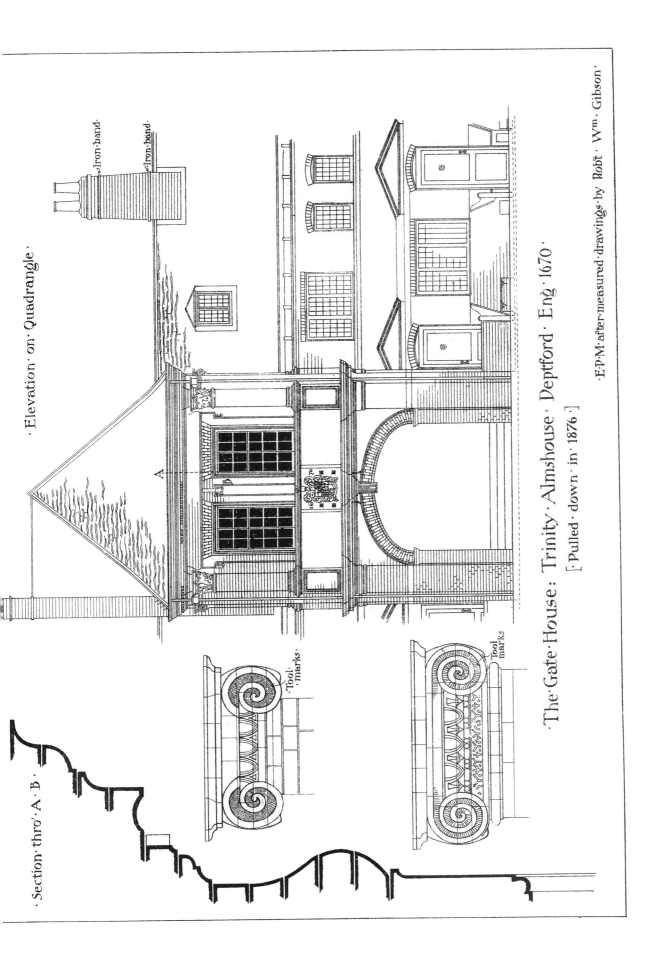

· Elevation · on · Quadrangle ·

· Iron · band ·
· Iron · band ·

· Section · thro' · A · B ·

· Tool · marks ·

· Tool · marks ·

· The · Gate · House : Trinity · Almshouse · Deptford · Eng · 1670 ·

[· Pulled · down · in · 1876 ·]

· E·D·M· after · measured · drawings · by · Robt · Wm · Gibson ·

· Hampton · Court · Palace :· Details · of · River · Front ·

Sir · Christopher · Wren   Architect

· Drawn · by · E · P · Morrill ·   · Measured · by · Hugh · P · G · Maule ·

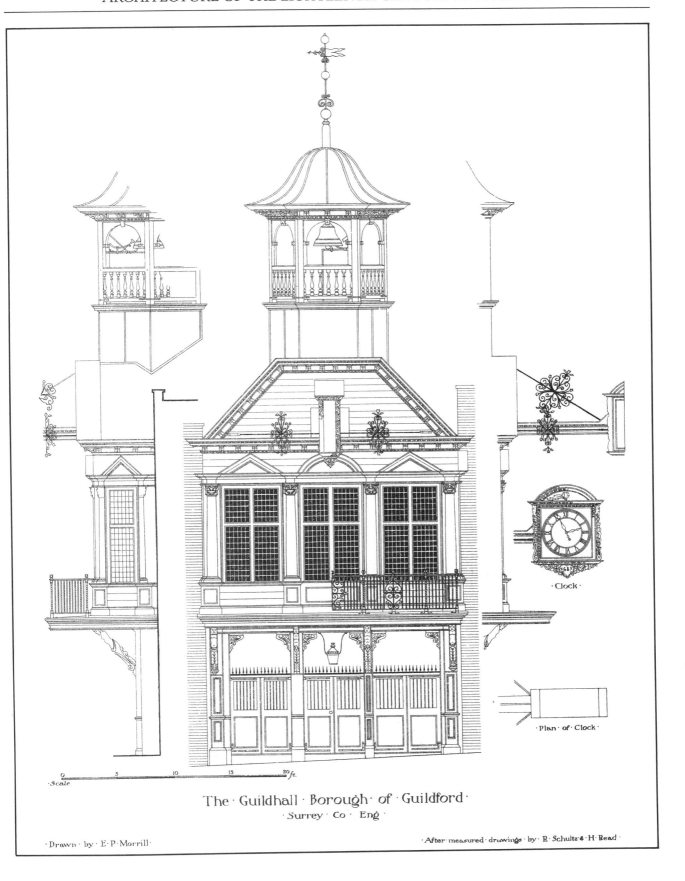

· Clock ·

· Plan · of · Clock ·

Scale

The · Guildhall · Borough · of · Guildford ·
· Surrey · Co · Eng ·

· Drawn · by · E · P · Morrill ·   · After · measured · drawings · by · R · Schultz · & · H · Read ·

TOWNSEND TOMB — 1760 — WITNEY, OXON, ENGLAND

TOMBS—1723—FAIRFORD CHURCHYARD, GLOUCESTERSHIRE, ENGLAND

Tomb (1769)

GRAVESTONES IN WITNEY CHURCHYARD, OXON, ENGLAND

TOMB—1711—WITNEY CHURCHYARD, OXON, ENGLAND

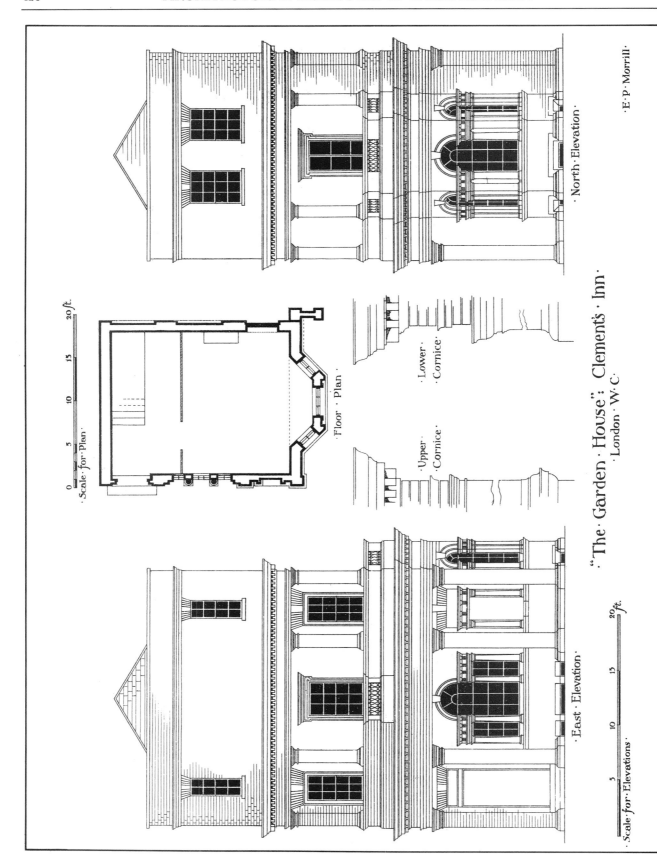

· North · Elevation ·

· E · P · Morrill ·

20 ft.

15

10

5

· Scale · for · Plan ·

0

· Floor · Plan ·

· Lower · Cornice ·

· Upper · Cornice ·

"· The · Garden · House" : · Clement's · Inn ·
· London · W · C ·

· East · Elevation ·

20 ft.

15

10

5

· Scale · for · Elevations ·

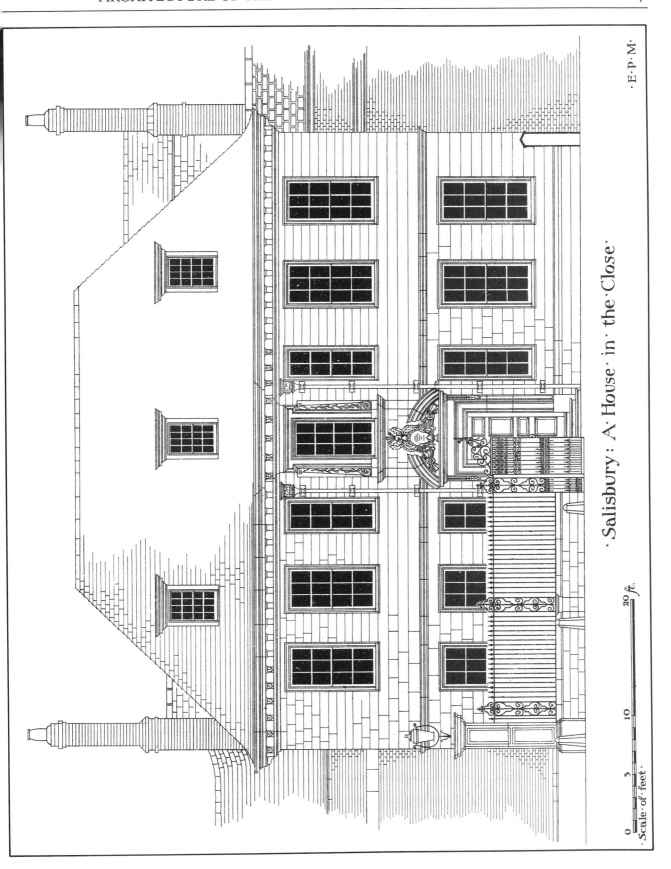

· Salisbury: A· House· in· the· Close·

· E· P· M·

· Scale· of· feet· 0 5 10 20 ft.

ENTRANCE GATE, BURFORD, OXON, ENGLAND

ENTRANCE GATE, EVESHAM, WORCESTERSHIRE, ENGLAND

ENTRANCE GATE AND PIERS, ST. GILES, OXFORD, ENGLAND

ENTRANCE GATE IN THE CLOSE, SALISBURY, ENGLAND

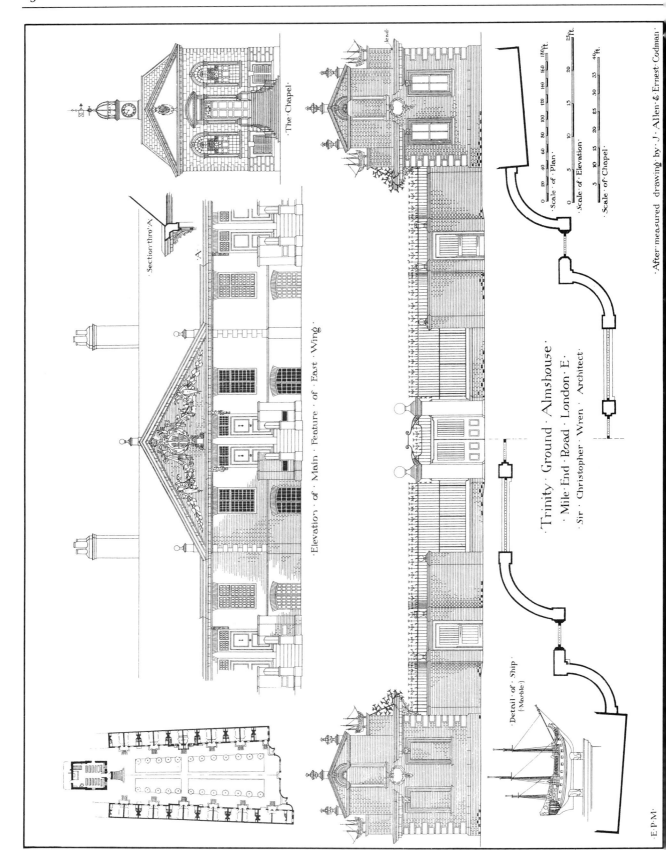

·The·Chapel·

·lead·

180·ft.
160
140
120
100
80
60
40
20
0
·Scale·of·Plan·

25·ft.
20
15
10
5
·Scale·of·Elevation·

40·ft.
35
30
25
20
15
10
5
·Scale·of·Chapel·

·After·measured·drawing·by·J·Allen·&·Ernest·Codman·

·Section·thro'·A·

·A·

·Elevation·of·Main·Feature·of·East·Wing·

·Trinity·Ground·Almshouse·
·Mile·End·Road·London·E·
·Sir·Christopher·Wren·Architect·

·Detail·of·Ship·
(·Marble·)

·E·P·M·

Photograph by T. W. Righton

A LAKE HOUSE

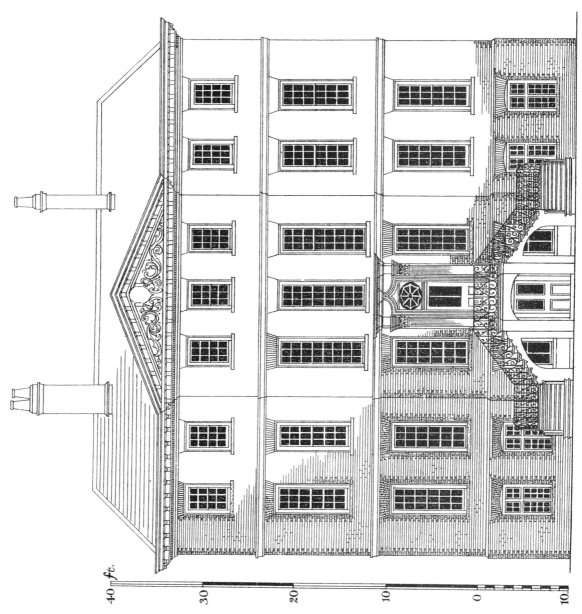

· North · Front ·

40 ft.

30

20

10

0

10

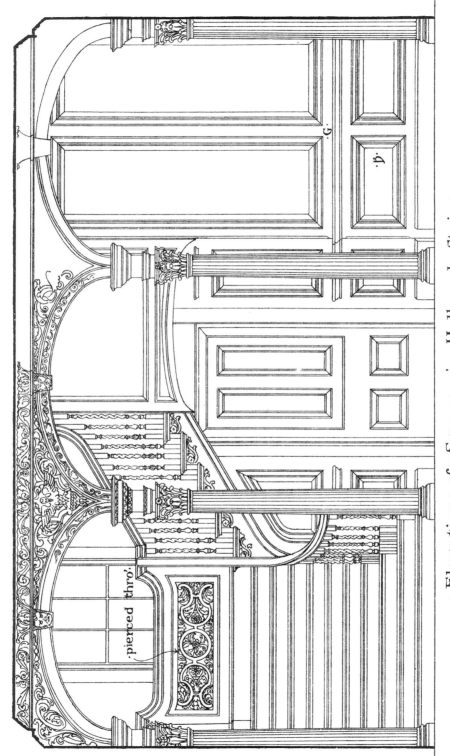

·pierced ·thro'·

·G·

·Φ·

· Elevation · of · Screen · in · Hall · and · Staircase ·

· The · Manor · House · Wandsworth · England
(·now destroyed·)

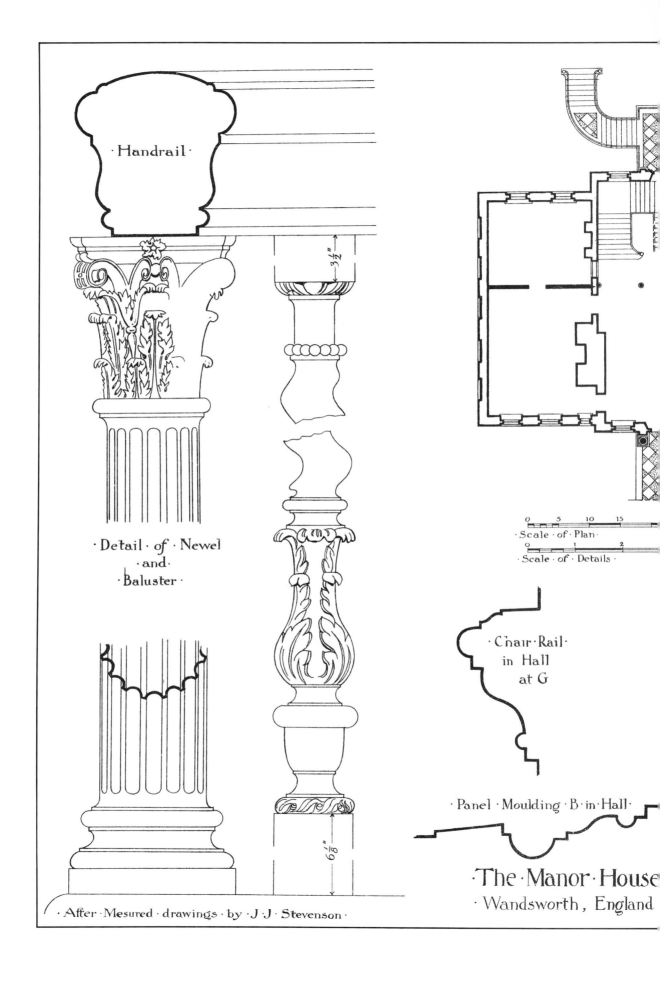

·Handrail·

·Detail · of · Newel ·
·and·
·Baluster·

$3\frac{1}{2}$"

$6\frac{1}{8}$"

·Scale · of · Plan·

·Scale · of · Details·

·Chair·Rail·
in Hall
at G

·Panel · Moulding · B · in · Hall·

·The·Manor·House
·Wandsworth, England·

·After·Mesured·drawings·by·J·J·Stevenson·

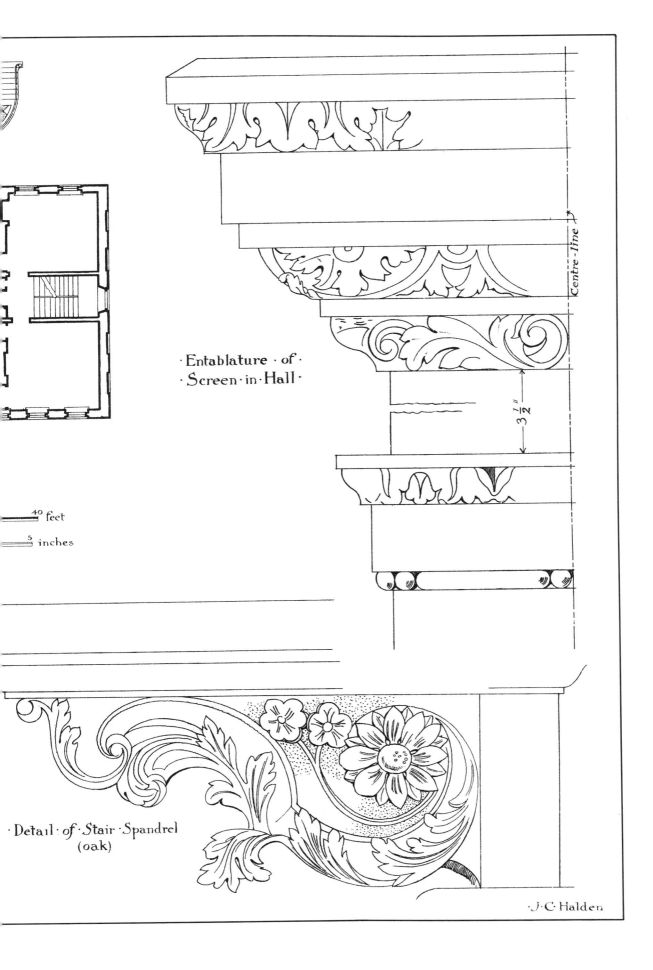

Entablature · of ·
· Screen · in · Hall ·

$3\tfrac{1}{2}''$

Centre-line

40 feet

5 inches

· Detail · of · Stair · Spandrel ·
(oak)

· J · C Halden

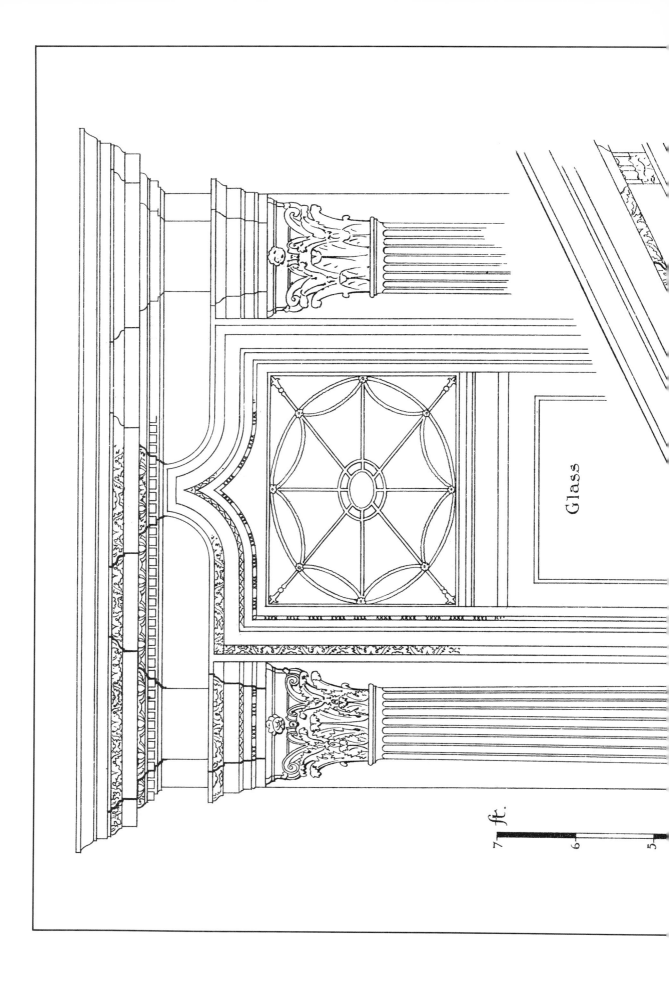

Glass

ft.

7

6

5

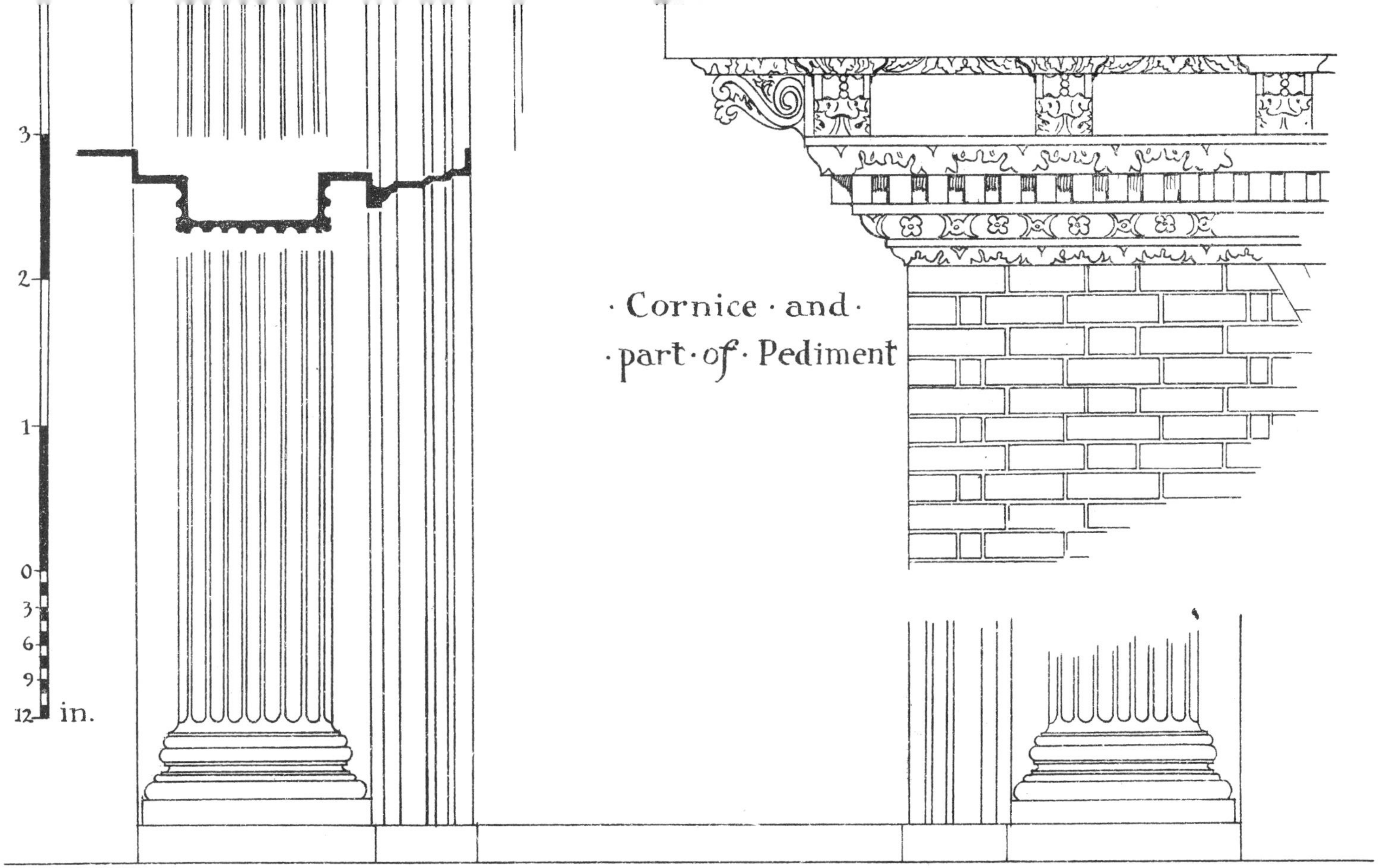

Cornice · and ·
· part · of · Pediment

· North · Entrance · Doorway ·

The · Manor · House · Wandsworth, England .

· Drawn · by · J · C · Halden

3

2

1

0
3
6
9
12 in.

COUNCIL CHAMBER, CHICHESTER, SUSSEX, ENGLAND

A Triad of Georgian Churches in London

Text by
Unknown Author
Originally published in 1900 as
Volume II of The Georgian Period

ST. MARY-LE-STRAND — 1714–1723 — LONDON

James Gibbs, Architect

A TRIAD OF GEORGIAN CHURCHES IN LONDON[1]

ST. MARY-LE-STRAND, 1714–1723

"ALTHOUGH the present building, of which Gibbs was the architect, was one of the fifty churches ordered to be built in certain populous localities, it represents a greater antiquity; for there had been an ancient church, not exactly on the same site, but at no greater distance from it. Stow calls it 'the parish church of the Nativity of our Lady and of the Holy Innocents of the Strand,' and further states that it was 'also known to some as the church of St. Ursula, from a brotherhood kept there.'

"Nearly the whole parish belonging to this church, together with the church itself and its churchyard, Chester's or Strand Inn and Worcester's Inn (belonging to the bishop of that see) and the tenements annexed, were all destroyed by the Protector Somerset, about the year 1549, and upon the levelled ground he built his stately palace, called Somerset House. The parishioners, being thus deprived of their church, had to go elsewhere, a state of affairs that lasted until 1713, when, the neighborhood having in the meanwhile become more populous, one of the first duties of the commissioners was to assign a new district, or parish, and build a church, to be named after the old church of St. Mary.

"The site chosen was in the widest part of the Strand, nearly opposite Somerset House, where the maypole, and in much earlier times a stone cross, had

stood. The maypole was moved a little farther westward, where it had but a short existence, for it was abolished five years afterwards. Sir Isaac Newton obtained possession of it from the inhabitants, and it found its way to Wanstead Park, where it became the support, or stand, for a large telescope.

"The new church, of which the foundation-stone was laid in 1714, was consecrated on January 1, 1723. Like Gibbs's work generally, it is almost pedantic in its close adherence to the rules of Classic art, and lacks the masculine vigor of Hawksmoor. It is a beautiful church, perhaps finer externally than internally, and its happy contiguity to Somerset House, together with its own commanding position, render it one of the most prominent and best seen of all the London churches, and it would be the grossest act of vandalism to remove it; yet, unhappily, more than one attempt to do so has been made. In plan it is a parallelogram, some 64 feet in length by 38 feet in width. The chancel, better developed in this than in many contemporary buildings, terminates eastward in an apse, and is flanked on each side, north and south, by two rather diminutive vestries. The arrangement at the west end is peculiar, for the tower is considerably broader from north to south than from east to west, and there are vestibules on each side (similar to the vestries at the other end), in one of which is placed the staircase giving access to the west gallery. The west door is preceded by a semi-circular porch or peristyle of Ionic columns. The floor of the church is well elevated above the street level, and a handsome flight of stone steps leads up to it, following the same lines as the porch.

"Externally, the church is of two orders — Ionic below and Corinthian above. Both have their proper en-

[1] Mr. Waterhouse's brief references in the preceding paper to the three great architects of the period, Wren, Gibbs and Hawksmoor, lead us to incorporate here the following extracts from Birch's *London Churches of the Seventeenth and Eighteenth Centuries*, together with their related illustrations. — WARE

tablature, the latter being finished on the north and south sides with alternate angular and circular pediments, and with a stone balustrade and vases, continued all round the building. The spaces between the columns on the upper stage have well-designed and well-proportioned windows, while the lower stage has semi-circular niches and no openings but to the vestibules, so as to shut out the sound of the street traffic as much as possible. The lower entablature is carried round the porch, which is finished by rather a flat half-domed top, carrying an urn. Originally a statue of Queen Anne stood on this half dome, but the statue was removed and the urn substituted not long after its erection. There is a tradition that this statue was again set up at Queen's Gate, Westminster, and in this new position was placed against the wall to conceal the fact that it was unfinished, the back being left in the rough only. A very sad accident, which led to fatal results, happened in connection with this church at the proclamation of peace by the heralds in 1802. Some people were on the roof of the church, and leaning on the parapet, when one of the vases gave way in consequence of improper dowelling, and fell on the heads of those below, killing two outright and two others eventually succumbing to their injuries. When officers were sent up to arrest him, the author of the catastrophe was found to have fainted from horror. The tower, which is shown so completely in the plate that a detailed description is unnecessary, has a very imposing appearance, when viewed from either the east or the west, but the reverse when seen from the north or south, as it is so much narrower on these sides. For this defect Gibbs is scarcely responsible, as when he designed the church it was intended to have a small western turret only, and a grand monumental column, 250 feet high, surmounted with a statue of Queen Anne, was to have been erected some 80 feet in front. The stone was actually obtained for this, but the queen died, and the commissioners fell back upon a design for a steeple to the church and, although the building had already advanced some 20 feet out of the ground, Gibbs had to work his existing walls in so as to carry the steeple.

"Considering the richness of the architecture employed externally, the interior is disappointing. The main ceiling is an ellipse, and is covered with small panels or coffers, groined over the windows, while the chancel ceiling, which is lower, is a semi-circle in section. The double order is also used internally, for the walls are in two divisions, and Corinthian pilasters, with Composite ones above, divide the church into bays, the lower parts of which are left blank, while the windows occupy the higher. The design to the entrance of the chancel is pleasing: it has coupled columns supporting a pediment, with the royal arms. The interior has been rearranged, the high pewing lowered, and the pulpit, originally placed in front of the chancel arch, moved to one side. Gibbs's estimate for his church was $8,997, but the total cost amounted to £16,341 1s 2d."

CHRIST CHURCH, SPITALFIELDS, 1715

"There had been in old times a small church and hospital in this locality, which had given the name to the adjacent fields, but it had long fallen to decay, and the fields were built over when, in 1715, the first stone of this fine church was laid, Nicholas Hawksmoor being the architect.

"Both for its plan and its architecture the church is unique. It is unlike any building of Wren's, although from Hawksmoor's association with him, one would have looked for some similarity, such as usually exists between the works of master and pupil. The chief peculiarity in the plan is the amount of space devoted to vestibules, lobbies, staircases and vestries, and the unusual distribution of the columns, for, although possessing nave and aisles, the colonnades dividing these are not treated continuously, either as regards the shape of the columns or the spaces, both the east and west bays being much the narrower. Two piers are introduced on each side to vary the monotony of the single columns. These piers have pilasters attached to the north and south sides, their use not being very apparent, as they carry nothing beyond a smaller pilaster on the side of the nave; this runs up to the flat ceiling, which, owing to its arrangement of panels, does not need support. The columns are of the Composite order, on high bases, carrying an entablature at right angles to the walls, a fashion introduced by Wren at St. James's Piccadilly, but which is more pleasingly carried out here by his pupil. From these entablatures spring the arches, which have squared coffered soffites; the arched ceilings of the aisles which follow the same curve, are divided into hexagonal panels, with circular flowers in each, an arrangement which gives to the arcade a deeply recessed appearance, and is certainly a very pleasing feature. The arcade has boldly moulded key-stones, and a moulded cornice, above which is the clerestory. The ceiling is very simple, being divided centrally into seven large panels, with smaller ones on each side, separated by flat bands of ornament, while circular flowers decorate the centre of each. The galleries, with the exception of the west one, have been removed, and this necessarily

CHRIST CHURCH—1715—SPITALFIELDS, LONDON
Nicholas Hawksmoor, Architect

gives an unmeaning look to the double tier of side windows—a bad effect much minimized by the upper range being circular. The most extraordinary departure from precedent consists in continuing the colonnade across the east and west ends, that at the west being broken in the centre by the introduction of the organ, while at the east end the entablature is carried across, and this screen of columns produces an effect which can only be described as 'scenic.' The chancel, behind this screen, is divided into two portions, the first of which has curved sides, narrowing it to a square recess, and all this part of the church, which should be the richest, is perfectly plain, with a flat plaster ceiling. The east window is of the Venetian type, and above this there is a semi-circular one. Internally the church was much altered many years ago, when the seats were lowered, and the galleries removed by the late Ewan Christian, and although it can be rarely said with regard to churches of this type that the removal of the galleries is an improvement, in this case it certainly was so. The old pulpit remains, but has been lowered, and the sounding-board is now suspended; the old brass branches have been utilized for gas-lights. Externally, the same extraordinary departure from all recognized rules makes this church very difficult to describe. The curious portico with its arched top, the extra width given to the east and west sides of the tower, which are prolonged so as to stand in advance of the side walls, and are brought back again to a square belfry-stage by inverted plain curved trusses, and the small arcaded stage supporting the octagonal spire, almost Norman in outline, are features which, combined, cause Christ Church, Spitalfields, to stand alone as a monument of architectural eccentricity; it is, after all, an eccentricity which pleases. The estimate for this church was £13,570, but the actual cost was £19,418 3s 6d."

CHRIST CHURCH, NEWGATE STREET, 1686–1687

"This church, the tower and spire of which is so conspicuous an object on the left-hand side of Newgate Street, is one of Wren's largest, but unfortunately not one of his finest. It occupies the site of the old Franciscan Friary Church, being built on the choir of that stately and magnificent edifice, which perished in the fire. The old church was usually known as the Greyfriars, and was the largest of the churches belonging to the mendicant orders, being over 300 feet in length. . . .

"After the fire, in which it was totally destroyed, Wren built the present church on the choir only of the ancient edifice, while the space where the nave stood was left as a churchyard. He built his columns and walls on the actual site of the older ones, and the proportions which suited the former fabric so well are not very happy in this. . . .

"The interior of this large and spacious church cannot be considered one of the happiest of Wren's efforts, but externally it possesses a beautiful tower, which, although shorn of its upper range of vases, the loss of which gives a pagodalike appearance to it, is still a very fine one. It is much to be regretted that these vases cannot be replaced, as they greatly helped the pyramidal effect. It is said that they had become dangerous, and were removed in consequence. The church was not rebuilt until 1686–1687, so that the parishioners had been without a church for over twenty years, during which time provision for divine worship seems to have been made by building a tabernacle among the ruins: interment still went on in the pavement of the present church, which is the ancient one, dated during this period."

CHRIST CHURCH — 1686–1687 — NEWGATE, LONDON
Sir Christopher Wren, Architect

NEWGATE PRISON ("OLD BAILEY") — 1770 — LONDON[1]
George Dance, Jr., Architect.

W. CURTIS GREEN DEL

[1] As Newgate Prison is just around the corner from Christ Church, as Dance was one of the noted architects of the time and as the structure itself is now vacant and on the point of being pulled down, we introduce here an illustration reproduced from a recent issue of the *Builder*. —WARE

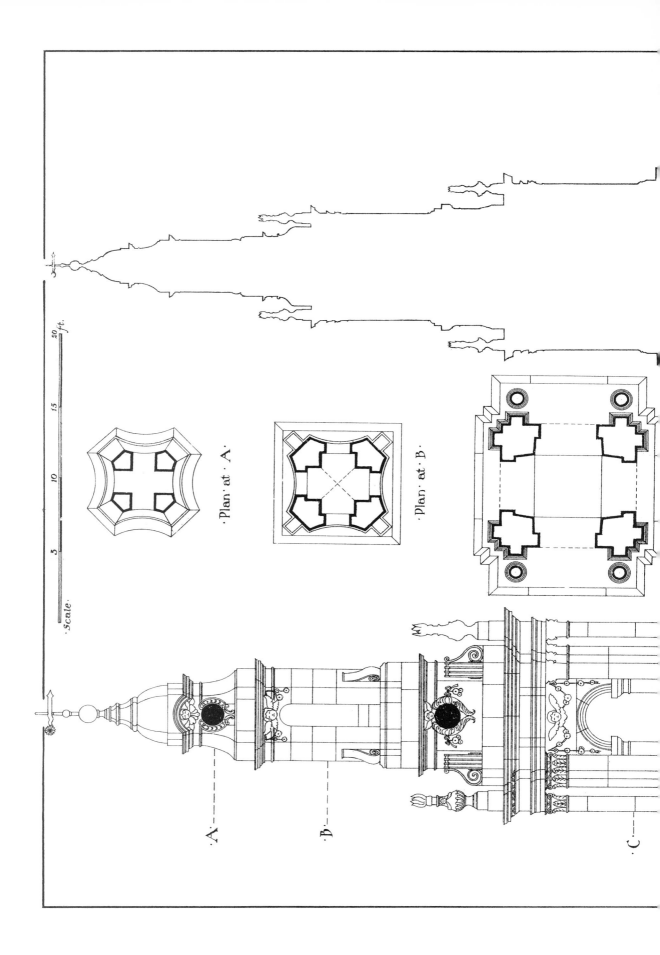

·Plan· at ·A·

·Plan· at ·B·

Scale.

·A·

·B·

·C·

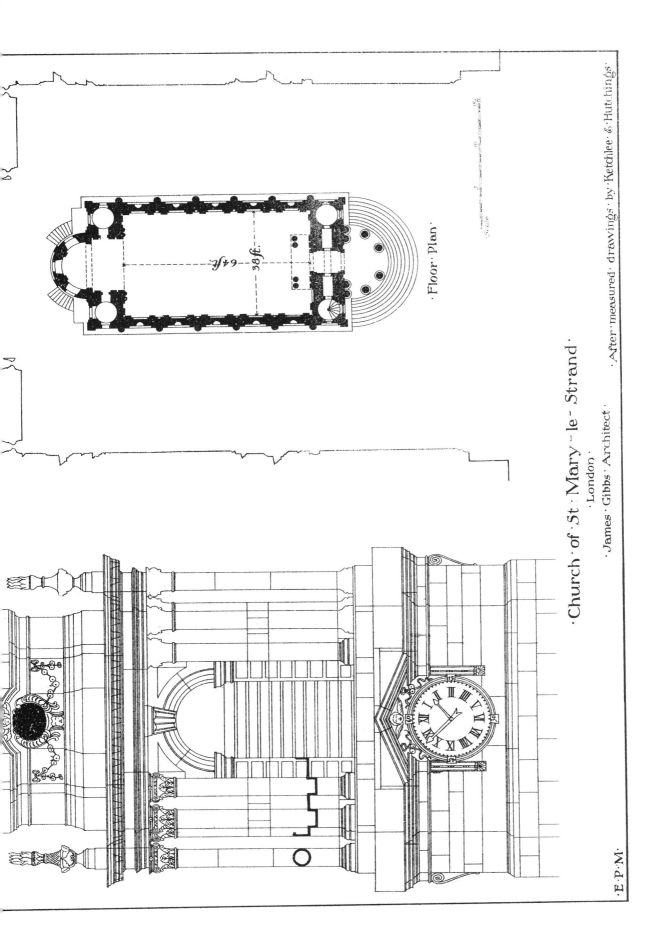

· Floor · Plan ·

38 ft.

64 ft.

· Church · of · St · Mary · - le - Strand ·
· London ·
· James · Gibbs · Architect ·   · After · measured · drawings · by · Ketchlee · & · Hutchings·

· E · P · M·

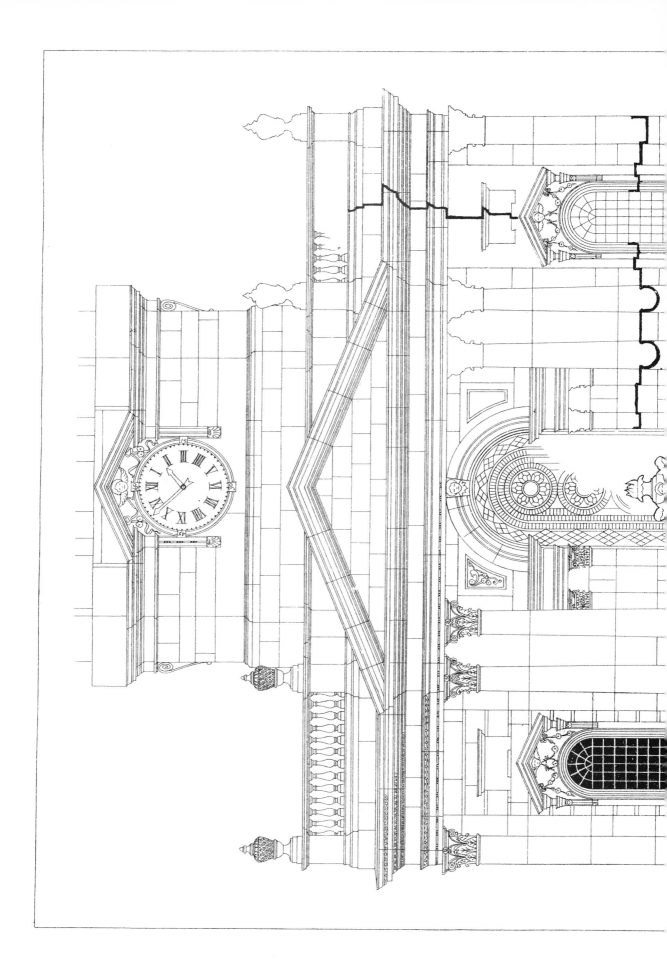

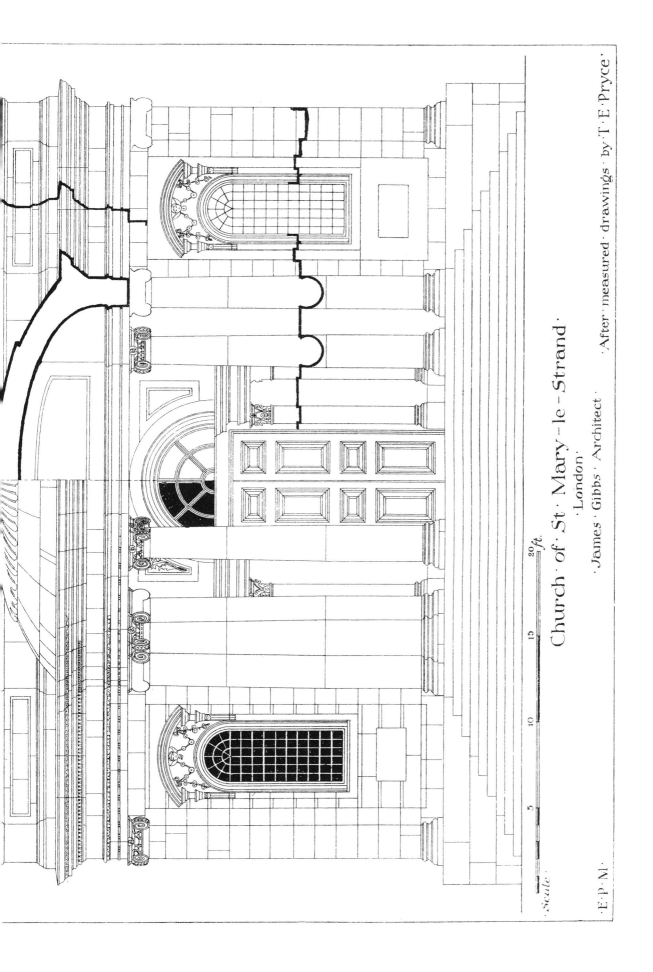

Church · of · St · Mary - le - Strand ·

·London·

·James · Gibbs · Architect ·

·After · measured · drawings · by · T · E · Pryce ·

·Scale·

5 10 15 20 ft.

·E·P·M·

Interior Looking East
CHRIST CHURCH, SPITALFIELDS, LONDON
Nicholas Hawksmoor, Architect

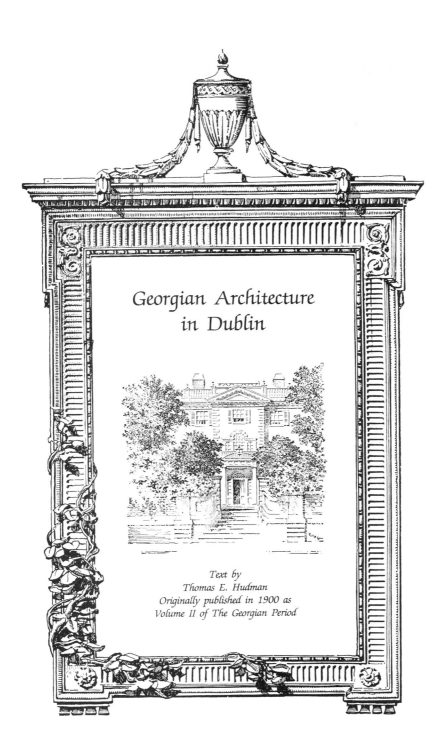

Georgian Architecture
in Dublin

Text by
Thomas E. Hudman
Originally published in 1900 as
Volume II of The Georgian Period

CUSTOMHOUSE — 1781 — DUBLIN.[2]

James Gandon, Architect

[2] The original cost of this building was about £560,000.

GEORGIAN ARCHITECTURE IN DUBLIN[1]

THE Four Georges have often been ridiculed and maligned, but I do not propose, in this chapter, to act as their defender or accuser. I have a simple and pleasing duty to perform, which is, to use their name and apply it to a period of architectural growth in Dublin which raised it from architectural poverty to comparative affluence in the art world. Dublin before the advent of the Georges was, so far as its buildings were concerned, a dead city and also a small city. In the year 1644 its population is given as 8,159, in 1777 as 137,208, in 1803 as 169,528. Although these figures are not altogether reliable, as they do not include any but adults, yet they are sufficiently so to show that the growth of the city was remarkable during the period, and show that it was indeed a golden age. Previous to this period many of its citizens had made their mark in history, but the city as a city was still in the mediaeval state, with narrow streets and a congested population, huddled together more for protection than comfort; but under the Georgian régime it blossomed into a truly metropolitan city, with wide streets and noble buildings, and became the pivot around which gathered a larger percentage of brilliant men than in any city of its size at the time. And as they were men of parts and enlightened views, they did not set about their work in any mean spirit. They did not enter upon their task by reforming the old city, but devoted their energies to making what was in reality a new city, trusting that the old town would by this means be relieved of its congestion and, by force of example, gradually fall into line with its new rival. How gloriously all this went on for a number of years and how it ended is now a matter of history which it is not my intention to go into, my province is to call attention to the glorious center of work in this city which we, as architects, cannot fail to admire, and be thankful that such men lived and used their opportunity to adorn our city with beautiful and enduring buildings that excite our admiration and are to us at once an ever-open book of instruction and a lasting memorial to their skill. It is true that this architectural outburst was not peculiar to Dublin, but it is also true that few cities can show as a result of such architectural renascence so many public and private buildings of such excellent taste and refinement.

The striking feature of Dublin is its wide line of streets and squares and the effect of its public buildings, so judiciously placed. The lines from College Green to Rutland Square would be hard to beat, not to mention Merrion Square, Fitzwilliam Square and St. Stephen's Green with their surrounding network of streets. The line of quays starting from the custom-house and finishing with the Phoenix Park was a magnificent conception. Unfortunately, the controlling influence over some of the buildings "en route" appears to have been relaxed, and the decadent period set in before the scheme was completed; but even now, under certain conditions of sky and atmosphere, the

---

[1] Mr. T. E. Hudman has been good enough to write out for us the address made by him in December, 1900, before the Architectural Association of London, and has also provided more illustrations than we can use, some the product of his own camera and others procured from Wm. Lawrence & Son, of Dublin.

WEAVER SQUARE, DUBLIN
Early Georgian

view, looking westward, from Carlisle Bridge is superb, both for color and architectural effect.

The building of the customhouse aided another fine effort in street planning by the formation of Gardiner Street, Mountjoy Square, North Great George's Street, Great Denmark Street, round about St. George's Church, and Eccles Street.

Another stroke of genius in city planning was the idea of the Circular Roads, North and South, by means of which the canals from the interior of the country were brought to encircle the city and terminate at the mouth of the river in shipping docks, and on each side of these canals were made wide roads, lined with rows of trees, thus forming a wide boulevard of about nine miles' circumference round the city, along which were built numerous fine houses; and although since then there have been numerous encroachments which injure this ideal thoroughfare, it still affords a pleasant promenade and has great artistic merits which remind one of Holland.

All this excellent work was due to the appointment of a Commission called the "Wide Streets Commission," which was originally called into being for the purpose of making a better means of communication from the Castle to the river, and so Parliament Street came into being. It was a small effort and its impor-

tance can hardly be judged at this period, as we have only very meager descriptions of the congested and inconvenient district around the Castle, but this Parliament Street evidently opened their eyes and led to the widening of Dame Street and the setting back of several of the houses in College Green, and ultimately to all the other lines of streets and squares.

This Commission was appointed by act of Parliament in 1757, and the act states its powers thus: "To open an avenue from His Majesty's Royal Palace to Essex Bridge," and certain persons were appointed by name to act as "Commissioners to make a wide and convenient street from Essex Bridge to the Castle of Dublin, to meet at such places as they think fit," and they were empowered to make a passage through such ground and to have the houses built on each side of the new street in whatever manner they should deem most eligible; they were further empowered to agree for the purchase of such ground with all the parties concerned, and, in case any refused to sell or show their title, then to summon a jury to inquire into the value, and assess the purchase money, for which the Commissioners were to give judgment conclusive, and, on paying the sum awarded, the premises were to be conveyed to them to build the street and sell and demise the surplus.

EARLY GEORGIAN HOUSES IN
CHAMBER STREET[3]

By subsequent act the Commissioners' powers were enlarged to other great plans of public utility. The funds by which the Commissioners were enabled to carry on their works were obtained by grants of money from Parliament and the imposition of a tax of one shilling per ton upon all coal imported into Dublin, and also a sum for card license and membership of all clubs.

When the Commissioners proceeded to exercise their powers they met with considerable opposition, as it is an Irishman's privilege to be "agin the Government," so it is recorded that "when the bargains for the Houses were concluded the inhabitants refused to quit the premises, alleging they had six months to remain, and prepared bills of injunction against the Commissioners. A host of slaters and laborers with ladders was secretly prepared on the night before the day on which the injunctions were to be filed, who proceeded in the first light of the morning to strip the roofs, and in a short time left the houses open to the sky. The terrified inhabitants bolted from their beds into the streets, under an impression that the city was attacked, of which there was some rumor, as it was a time of war. On learning the cause, they changed their bills of injunction into bills of indictment," which apparently were of no effect, for the record continues, "but the Commissioners proceeded without further impediment." As far as I can find out, the works carried out by these Commissioners amounted to over £750,000, and if to this we add the cost of the quay walls (which were the work of the Port and Dock Boards), the Circular Roads and the various buildings, public and private, there is no doubt that many million pounds of money were spent in building work during the fifty or sixty years of activity, and it is little wonder if Dublin assumed a prosperous air and appeared, as it was in reality, a metropolis. It is interesting to note that in spite of the great changes and improvements taking place in what may be called the new, or outer, Dublin of that day, how little the old city changed, and so remains to this day. It is still the most wretched and congested part of the city, and neglect and decay are the only agents at work removing the old houses. In a few years there will be left few, if any, of the picturesque old houses, which are so agreeable to behold, mainly for the artistic pleasure they give.

The efforts of the Government of that day did not end with simply widening streets. Philanthropy had

---

[3] The brick fronts are now coated with plaster, pebble-dashed, the plastering being now more or less in disrepair.

WEAVER HALL IN THE COOMBE[4]

its share of their patronage. They supported private benevolence in founding hospitals and other similar institutions, and many of these hospitals, as Sir Patrick Dunn's, Mercers', the Rotunda and the Coombe remain practically the same to this day; others have been removed to other sites, but still we must credit the Georgian period with the founding of nearly all our charitable institutions.

As for the architecture of the period, there is a noticeable change in treatment from the earlier Georgian to the middle and later period. I might almost say that the advent of the "Wide Street Commissioner" was the starting point for reverting to the Italian and Classic methods. Previous to this there is a strongly marked Dutch feeling about all the buildings: a purely brick style, with gables of brick and brick strings, and, later the introduction of stone strings and blocking-courses. In Sweeney's Lane there exists a group of three houses the date of which is carved in a brick panel on the gable as 1721, which, although in a dilapidated condition, is one of our best examples of the earlier style, and its moulded brick courses can still

be clearly traced. In Chambers Street and Weavers' Square and several other streets there are still many of these earlier houses, but the mouldings have gone, and only the lines remain.

In the Weavers' Hall, in the Coombe House, in Ward's Hill and the old Deanery, we have examples of the beginning of the later types, with the introduction of the stone blocking courses and moulded stone windowsills, and in these houses we find greater attention paid to the hall and staircase; the walls are paneled in wood, the staircase is wider, the balusters are more elaborate and better turned, the cartouche brackets are frequently carved, newel posts disappear, and we have continuous handrails with large scroll-endings and curtail steps. Fireplaces receive more attention, and in every detail it is evident that money was becoming more plentiful, bringing with it the usual results.

One of the causes of decay in these earlier houses is the defective make of the bricks of which they were

[4] The original cornice and pediment has been replaced by a brick parapet. The central niche contains a statue of George II.

HOUSES IN SWEENEY'S LANE[5]

built. I don't know where they were made, as I can find in old histories no mention of Dublin brickfields, but I know that the stock bricks of which Merrion Square and many other like houses are built were made from clay taken from the fields of Merrion; there were also brickfields near Sutton, and, judging from some bricks which I have seen, and which were known to have been made there, I should say that the facing-bricks of the earlier houses came from them. The few moulded bricks used were, I think, imported, as those existing bear evidence of being made of a more sandy clay than we have in Ireland.

The great charm of the earlier work is its simplicity, and even now, in its picturesque state of old age and decay, it still has valuable lessons for the architectural student who cares to study them.

But in the middle and later period we find a totally different type of work: ambition to excel is the key-note. The public buildings are ambitious, without doubt, but fortunately the men who designed them were capable, and the result is satisfactory. The group of architects, or, rather, the best of them, who prac-

ticed in Dublin deserve to be known, and I give their names: J. Smith, Cassels, Thomas Cooley, James Gandon, Sir William Chambers, Sproule, Ensor, F. Johnston, Wilkins, Murray.

Cassels was a German. His greatest work in Dublin was Leicester House, built for the Duke of Leicester. It is now the headquarters of the Royal Dublin Society, and is the center of a group of buildings forming the National Museum Library and Picture Gallery. Tyrone House, for the Earl of Tyrone, in Marlborough Street, is another of his works: it is now in use as the Central National School of Dublin. Several houses in Henrietta Street are also of his design.

Thomas Cooley was in his early youth a carpenter, but by study he became proficient in design and, entering the competition, he was awarded first premium for the new Royal Exchange,[6] Dublin (now the City

[5] These houses, of the early Georgian period, bear in the gable the date 1721.

[6] This building, now the city hall but originally the Exchange erected in 1796 by a company of merchants, was won in competition by Thomas Cooley and formed his introduction to Dublin practice.

ROTUNDA HOSPITAL[7] (1751)

KING'S INNS (1776)
James Gandon, Architect

Hall). His other important works are Tower Armagh Cathedral, Newgate Prison, Dublin, and several other prisons and court houses and the Four Courts, Dublin.

James Gandon first began his architectural career as an assistant to Sir William Chambers, and afterwards became his pupil. He commenced practice in London, and his first essay in Dublin was in the competition for the Royal Exchange, in which he was placed second to Cooley. Afterwards he came to Dublin and was commissioned to design the Customhouse. Upon the death of Cooley, he finished the Four Courts and he also designed the original Carlisle Bridge, the King's Inns and a portion of the Bank of Ireland. He was a cultured man and a very capable etcher. He evidently modeled his work upon that of his master, Sir William Chambers, whose work his much resembles in its gracefulness and pleasant grouping. He was a man of passionate impulse, and it is recorded of him that during a period of absence a portion of the Customhouse had been erected that did not please him, so he collected a body of laborers and marched them to the work in the early morning and pulled the offending work down before the contractors' men arrived.

Sir William Chambers designed the greater part of Trinity College, Charlemont House (now the Register Office), Aldborough House (now the Army Service Stores), and several other residences. It is not certain if Sir William Chambers ever was in Dublin, and it is believed that the supervision of his work was entrusted to some of his best pupils, as two of them remained here and practiced as architects. Sproule was one of them. His principal work consisted of at least half of the houses in Merrion Square.

Francis Johnston was born in Ireland and began practice in Armagh in 1786, afterwards practicing in Dublin. He was a man of great skill and refinement and designed the Castle Chapel, St. George's Church, the General Post Office and part of the Bank of Ireland. He bought the ground upon which the Royal Hibernian Academy of Arts stands, erected the present building and picture galleries and partly endowed it at a total cost to himself of £14,000.

Wilkins was a graduate of Cambridge University and was introduced to Dublin as the architect for the Nelson Monument in Sackville Street.

Murray was a Dublin man and his only known public building is the College of Surgeons[9] in St. Stephen's Green.

It is curious to note that most of the public buildings erected by architects who received their early training in England have their dressed stonework executed in Portland-stone — an excellent white freestone from the Portland stone-quarries in the south of England — to the exclusion of the splendid materials which are to be had in the neighborhood of Dublin. I mean the granite of the Dublin hills and the blue limestone obtainable in the north of the county. Probably, until the advent of these architects, stone-masons were neither plentiful nor skillful, and therefore builders had to import men from England who would only be accustomed to the softer building-stones in use there and could not work the harder granite and the still harder blue limestone. But finally, during the later Georgian period, we find granite freely used for

---

[7] See photo on page 174. This view shows not only the main building designed by Cassels but also the Rotunda itself designed by Ensor, originally built for and still used as an assembly-hall and concert-room to increase the revenues of the Hospital.

[8] This building was designed by Thomas Cooley but was finished by James Gandon. The central portion was intended to set back, but lack of space forced it forward, to the injury of the effect of the group.

[9] This building was designed by Murray, whose son and grandson — the latter still living — have practiced architecture in Dublin.

FOUR COURTS — 1776–1786 — DUBLIN, IRELAND[8]

Thomas Cooley, Architect

OLD PARLIAMENT HOUSE, NOW BANK OF IRELAND [10]

columns and capitals and moulded work of the finest kind.

The blacksmiths of the period were excellent craftsmen, and around many of the private houses of the time there still exist some charming lamp-irons, both standard and arched, and also square pedestals of iron with scroll-fillings at the ends and corners of the fore-court railings.

The general character of the private houses was that of a brick box, with square holes for windows. The quaintness of the early period seems to have been ignored, and architectural effort is exhausted in the entrance, which has all the character of the period. Internally the houses are remarkable for the elegance and refinement of their detail. Some wise and knowing men imported from Italy a band of clever workmen who were also artists: these men embellished the ceilings of hundreds of houses with the most delightful designs in plaster work, most of it modeled *in situ*; but it is only in a few that it remains today, showing its delicate modeling still unclogged by the distemper of the inevitable whitewasher. These men were very cunning in the designing and working of marble chimney-pieces and in the inlaying of them with colored marbles; one of the band, named Bossi, was especially so, and, as the secret of his word died with him, anyone possessing a mantelpiece of his work has a work of art which can be sold at any time for several hundreds of pounds, so much prized are they. I am sorry to say that the monetary needs of many of the property owners of Dublin and also their apathy in matters of art has led many of them to denude their houses of many of these art treasures and sell them to the many eager buyers

from other countries. But I am glad to notice that the Government have intervened in several instances and purchased them for the National Museum, so that although they do not adorn their original positions they remain with us, and can be admired and studied.

The joinery of these houses is also of excellent workmanship; its design is "on all fours with" the work of the period, the mouldings have numerous small members, and in the best houses all the principal doors are of mahogany, a wood which at that period was new, very expensive, and consequently just the material for the ostentatious display of wealth.

In looking over some of the old Dublin newspapers of the period, one comes across some curious and interesting paragraphs, as, for example, the following advertisement in the *Dublin Chronicle,* 1787: —

CURIOUS LOCKS, PATENT WATER-CLOSETS, ETC., AT
NO. 62 CAPEL STREET, DUBLIN.

Robert Mallet respectively acquaints the Nobility, Gentry and Architects and others that he is the only manufacturer in this Kingdom of the following articles, viz. I. Patent locks for doors, cabinets, etc., on a principle entirely new without wheels or wards and so perfectly secure as to defy the utmost efforts of art and ingenuity to open them. II. Patent water-closets which act with valves and may be fixed in bedrooms, dressing-rooms,

---

[10] The Old Parliament House, now the Bank of Ireland, was erected at three different epochs: the central portion, attributed to Cassel but real author unknown, was built first. The portico on the right was the entrance to the House of Lords and that portion of the building was designed by Gandon. The remainder of the building, by Johnston, the architect of the General Post Office, was built after the Union. Foley's statue of Grattan in front faces Trinity College.

TRINITY COLLEGE, DUBLIN
Sir Wm. Chambers, Architect

or any other part of the house without being in the least incommodious or offensive. III. Sundry hydrostatical machines for raising water from any depth and carrying it to any given height to supply houses, extinguishing fires, etc., also a flight machine for escaping from fire from a window or wall or any height; any number of persons may descend in the securest manner by the same machine.

We of the present day are very well accustomed to strikes and combinations of workmen, but from the following extract from the *Dublin Chronicle* of 1787 it would appear to be nothing new: —

"Our working artisans, too much prone to combination and outrage, have uniformly set their faces against every improvement or extension of their respective branches. At present the calico-printers without a shadow of reason or justice are proceeding to the most unwarrantable lengths. The cause which they assign for their illegal conduct is an aggravation of their guilt.

"They allege that it is contrary to the established rules of their business to increase the number of hands and therefore will not permit a single apprentice to to be taken beyond the number they think proper,"

and later the same paper says: —

"There are at this time thirteen houses in this city where the working people of the different branches assemble at different stated periods, in order to support the pernicious cause of combination. It would perhaps be a very judicious and prudent measure to withdraw the license for selling malt and spirituous liquors from every publican against whom it could be proved that he or she harboured such illegal meetings, or, as they are termed, committees, in his or her place. These men who are chosen by the aggregate body of the working people of each branch are for the most part artful and designing fellows who levy contribution on the rest and live in a state of idleness and dissipation themselves. Then to promote a spirit of combination and to enjoy the plunder of the deluded persons whom they both dupe of their money and lead into acts highly injurious to themselves and the trading interests of the Kingdom. . . ."

These extracts show that even at that time there was the same kind of strife going on between capital and labor as in the present day, but it also shows that there must have been considerable commercial activity, since, as we know in our time, it is in times of trade activity that we suffer most from these disturbances.

It is a fact that the master-minds in control at this period were very active in promoting every possible enterprise that would advance the trade and commerce of the country, and inducements were held out to induce skilled workmen to migrate to Dublin, to work and instruct the people in various new trades and industries, and prizes were frequently offered for designs in textile fabrics. So for many years there was great prosperity, and, as appears by the trade reports of the time, there was a steadily growing business in exporting manufactured goods: even to this day the old silverplate manufactured in Dublin during the Georgian period is eagerly sought after by collectors and museums, and frequently realizes as much as forty shillings per ounce.

Altogether, Dubliners can look back with pride to the Georgian period. Its governors managed their business so well that they created a new and truly metropolitan city which attracted to its centre a brilliant crowd of the most clever men in the Kingdom, who were satisfied to remain here and work for its good, and the citizens of Dublin of that day could say, as did the men of an older city, that they were citizens of "no mean city."

CASINO AT CLONTARF

This little building, designed by Sir William Chambers, stands in the grounds of Lord Charlemont's place, Clontarf. It is extremely fine in detail, but has been allowed to fall into disrepair. Lord Charlemont's house is now used as a convent. See photograph on page 175.

BLUE-COAT SCHOOL, 1773

This building has never been finished, as the guardians were extravagant and squandered their funds. Efforts are now being made to have the tower finished under the charge of Sir Thomas Drew after the original drawings. See photograph on page 178.

VIEW FROM CORK HILL

In the background rises the "Bedford Tower" in the Upper Castle Yard; on the left is a portion of the city hall, while at the right is Lord Essex's house, now used as municipal offices and still containing some fine plasterwork and handsome mahogany doors. See photograph on page 177.

CITY HALL — 1796 — DUBLIN
Thomas Cooley, Architect

· Doorway · in Rutland · Square ·

· Doorway · in · Upper · Merrion · St ·

· Houses · in · St · Stephen's · Green ·

Middle · Georgian · Period ·]

· Doorway · in · Merrion Square ·

· Later · Georgian · Doorways ·
· in · Dublin ·

· Doorway · in · Leeson · St · Dublin ·

ROTUNDA HOSPITAL—1751—DUBLIN
Cassels, Architect

THE CASINO, CLONTARF, NEAR DUBLIN
Sir Wm. Chambers, Architect
[Not the Temple Marino]

The "Bedford Tower"
DUBLIN CASTLE, DUBLIN, IRELAND

CORK HILL, DUBLIN, IRELAND

BLUE-COAT SCHOOL—1773—DUBLIN

COLLEGE OF SURGEONS, ST. STEPHEN'S GREEN, DUBLIN

W. Murray, Architect

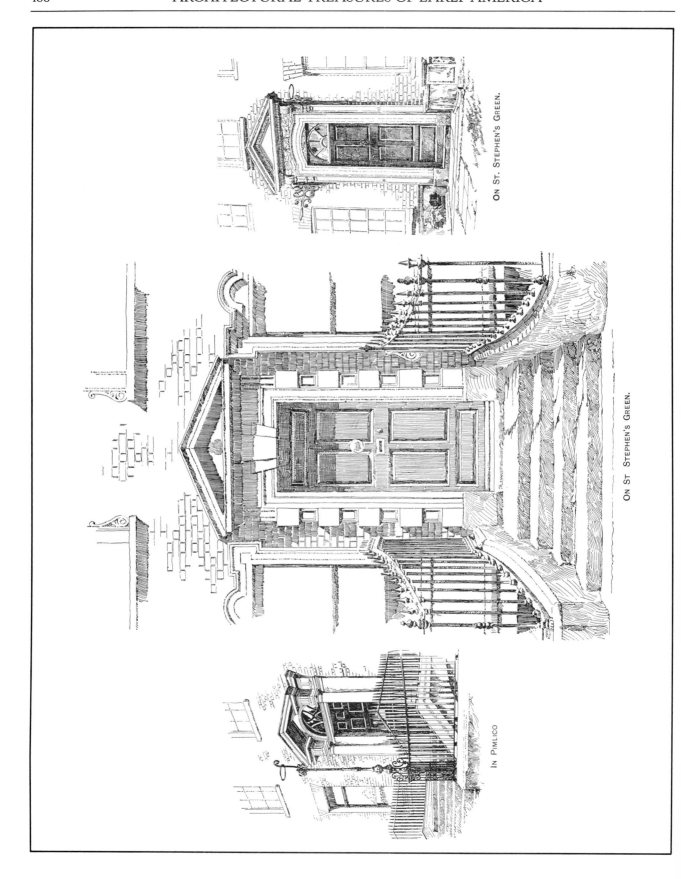

On St. Stephen's Green.

On St Stephen's Green.

In Pimlico

The Men Who Designed Old Colonial Buildings

Text by
George Clarence Gardner
Originally published in 1902 as
Volume III of The Georgian Period

Door in Vestibule
CITY HALL, NEW YORK, NEW YORK
John McComb, Architect

THE MEN WHO DESIGNED THE OLD COLONIAL BUILDINGS

ONE of our architectural writers in comparing Gothic architecture with that of the Renaissance makes the point that it was in the latter style that the individuality of the architect appeared, that all Gothic work by its strength and vigor completely swept away any personality, however strong, which the designer or designers might possess. Whether this is really true or not, or whether the fact that the chief knowledge of the architectural monuments of Northern Europe of the Gothic period rests on only slight historical foundation, as regards names and dates, while that of the Renaissance is generally reinforced by pretty accurate records of the men who did the work, may not be responsible, or whether it is simply that we do not understand the characteristics of the Gothic works as well; or whatever may be the reason, it is undoubtedly true that the architectural student can determine with much greater accuracy from certain peculiarities of construction and decoration the probable designers of buildings of the Renaissance period. The work of Brunelleschi, of Michelozzi, or Alberti, of Palladio, or of their several schools can be pretty definitely determined by a more or less careful examination of the work, and often a building shows distinctly the stamp of an individual; but while Gothic work varies in localities and shows for varying localities certain distinctly marked characteristics, I am not aware that even M. Viollet-le-Duc is dogmatic when it comes to ascribing the work of the great French cathedrals to this or that mastermind.

Even the debased Renaissance architecture, which it was our fortune as colonists here in America to receive from the mother country, debased through the era, still more debased through English influence; even in this architecture, which our ancestors brought with them and which had at times become so thoroughly formal as to admit of hardly any strength of character, the personality of the men combined with their environment resulted in many cases in the expression of certain individual peculiarities, which make it possible to distinguish the work of some of the earlier men apart from the testimony of town records and family genealogy.

Strictly speaking, up to the beginning of the nineteenth century, I know of no architects in America; but, if various records and histories speak truly, fully 100 years before this time plans and elevations of buildings were prepared and drawn for the distinct purpose of either imitating or improving upon English models, and the men who did this may be divided into two types, the carpenter-architect and the amateur architect.

Of the first type, the carpenter-architect, Asher Benjamin is a good example, though his work was confined chiefly to comparatively unimportant buildings. He began as a carpenter working in Greenfield, Deerfield, and the surrounding Massachusetts towns. He published a book at Greenfield of the "simple and practical" type; then he went to Boston, practiced there and published two or three more works on architecture of a much more pretentious sort, and died comparatively a poor man, as all good architects should. Of the other example, the "amateur" architect, Thomas Jefferson, from his station in life, is cer-

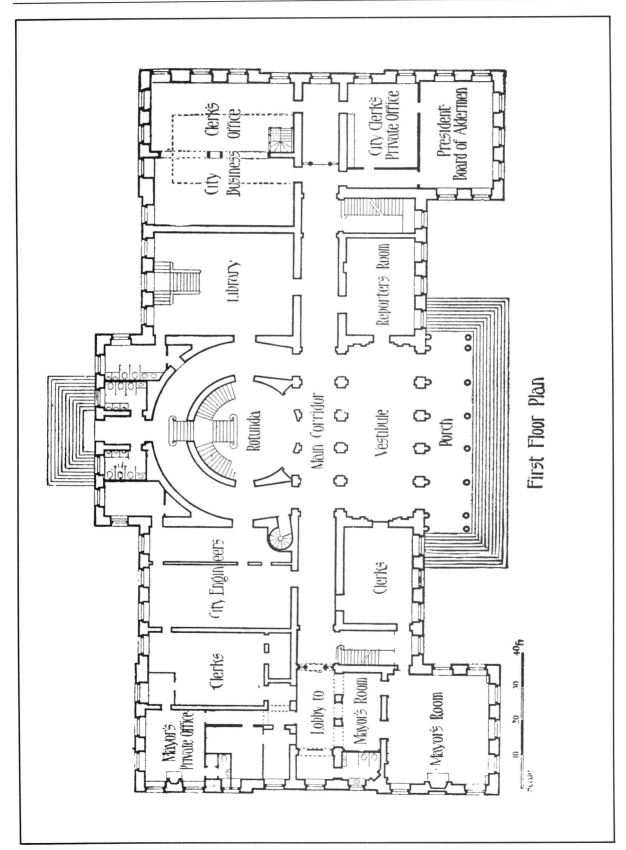

CITY HALL, NEW YORK, NEW YORK

John McComb, Architect

First Floor Plan

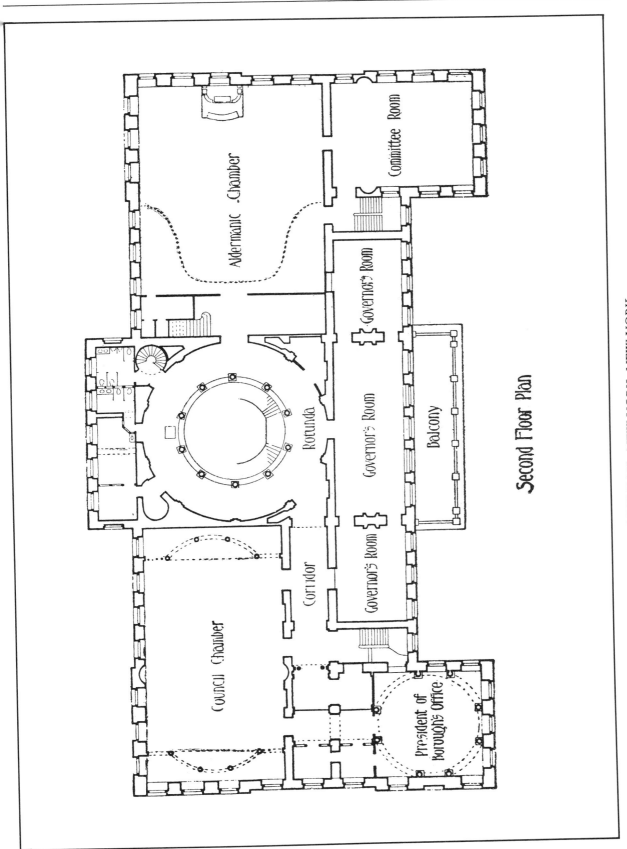

Second Floor Plan

CITY HALL, NEW YORK, NEW YORK
John McComb, Architect

Gateway
THOMAS COWLES PLACE,
FARMINGTON, CONNECTICUT

tainly the most notable example. His work from his famous "four-inch wall" built in a wavy line, so it should not tip over, to the schemes for the University of Virginia are too well known to need more than passing mention. Both of the examples quoted are, however, of rather a late period. Of the seventeenth-century work the greater part owes its architectural features to the carpenter-architect and, I am inclined to think, to some book of plates. Of course, many of these earlier men had not even this aid; in fact, a good many examples of the work in districts more remote from the larger towns show plainly that the decorated pediments over front doors, cornices, and pilaster caps are worked out from memory or tradition, for the execution of the work is too good to lay the peculiarities of the finished product to lack of ability to carry out the desired effect.

There are even now, in libraries, in garrets and in the possession of a few book collectors, works published, largely in England and some in America, during the eighteenth century manifestly intended for the aid of the carpenter and usually advertising on the title page this fact in convincing and often amusingly ingenuous language.

John Allis, born in Braintree in 1642, who married a widow and had eleven children and who came to Hat-

field from Springfield in 1661, is one of the earliest of these carpenter-architects of whom I have been able to find any record. He designed the first church in West Springfield, built in 1668, and the churches in Hatfield and in Hadley. I say he designed them, for the records of the old First Church in West Springfield indicate that aesthetic effect was sought for by the builder even though he was at the same time a contractor. Much of the ornamental work he personally executed.

At New London, John Elderkin, who came to that town from Lynn in 1651, built the meeting house and the parsonage and probably was called upon to aid in the designing of many of the older houses in southeastern Connecticut. Old account books, church records and journals mention these earlier men almost invariably as builders. At times the church committees give directions, more or less explicit, as to the architectural style which the building shall follow, usually a copy of some building of greater or less notoriety.

Richard Munday built the town hall at Newport in 1783. John Smibert is responsible for Faneuil Hall, in Boston. Peter Banner did the Park Street Church in Boston, and at the head probably of these men stands Peter Harrison, who undoubtedly had received in England more or less of a technical education in architecture. He is said to have been of assistance to Sir John Vanbrugh and a pupil of James Gibbs's, and his admirers feel that he should be placed in a different rank from the other men of his time. Whether he derived his income solely from the making of plans or not, I do not know. Unless he did I see no reason why he should not be classed with the amateur architects or the carpenter-architects.

In New York, one McBean, who lived in New Brunswick, New Jersey, designed in 1764 St. Paul's Chapel. It is possible that he was a pupil of Gibbs's,

HOUSE IN PROVIDENCE, RHODE ISLAND

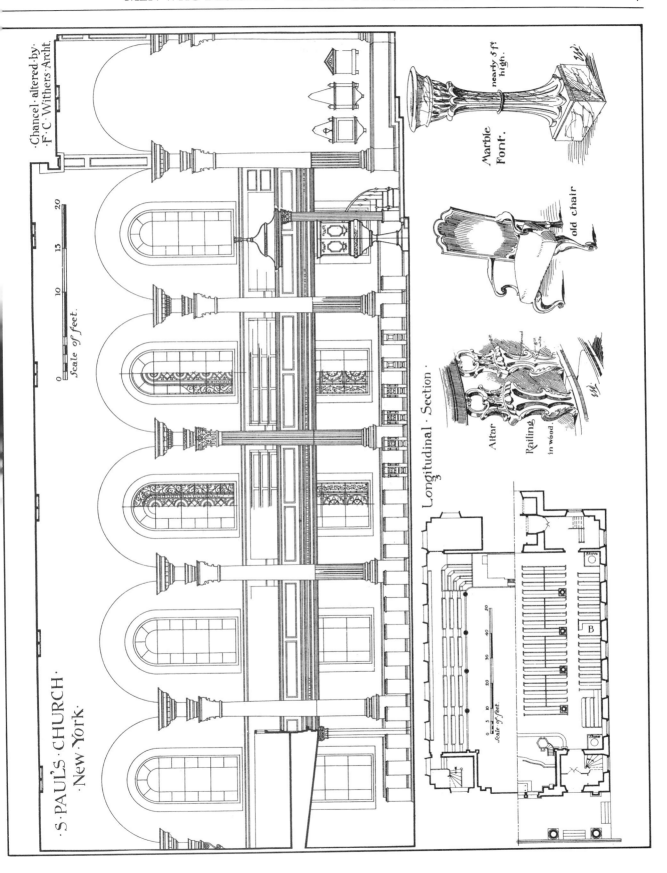

·Chancel· altered· by·
·F·C· Withers· Archt·

·S· PAUL'S· CHURCH·
·New· York·

Scale of feet.
0   5   10   15   20

Marble
Font.

nearly 3 f.t
high.

old chair

Altar
Railing
in wood.

Longitudinal · Section ·
3

Scale of feet.
0 5 10   20   30   40   50

Stove

B

Stove

ST. JOHN'S CHAPEL, VARICK STREET, NEW YORK CITY

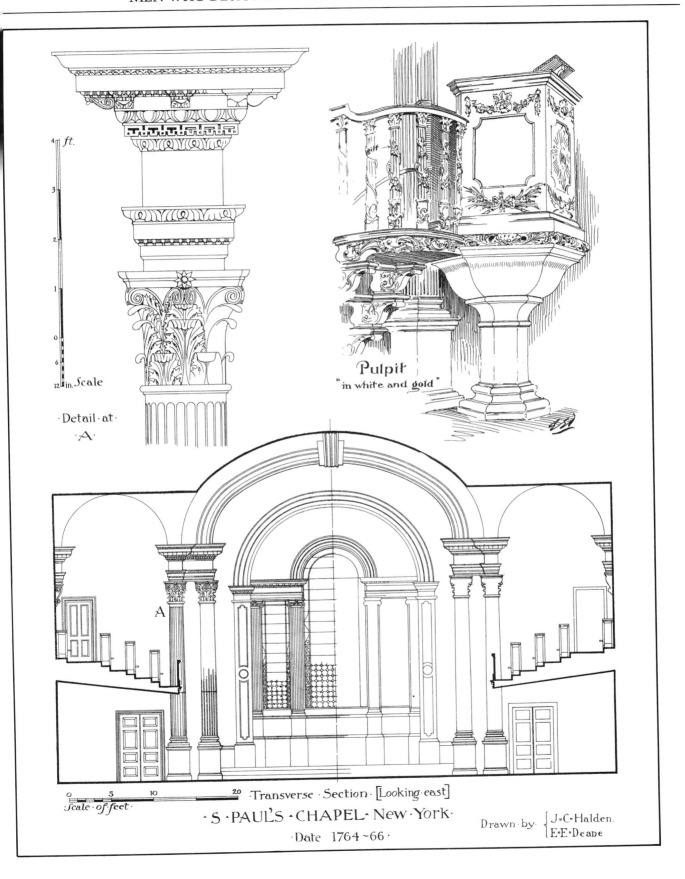

4 ft.

3

2

1

0

6

12 in. Scale

·Detail·at·
·A·

Pulpit
"in white and gold"

A

0   5   10   20 ·Transverse·Section·[Looking·east]
·Scale·of·feet·

·S·PAUL'S·CHAPEL·New·York·
·Date 1764~66·

Drawn·by· { J·C·Halden.
{ E·E·Deane

SOUTH CHURCH, SALEM, MASSACHUSETTS
Samuel McIntire, Architect

HOUSE ON BENEFIT STREET, PROVIDENCE,
RHODE ISLAND

but it is more probable that drawings of Gibbs's work furnished him with his inspiration.

In Farmington, Connecticut, Judah Woodruff, a man prominent in the town affairs, was the leading builder of Western Connecticut. He designed the church at Farmington, which, by the way, is a free copy of the one in Wethersfield. He designed and built a dozen of the fine old houses of which Farmington now is justly proud, and he, like John Allis, of Hatfield, executed much of his own designing, the capitals of the pulpit and an elaborately carved sounding-board having been done by his own hand. (Some of the best Colonial festoons decorating a window-cap that I ever saw, by the way, a lady in Old Hadley told me "grandpa" had himself cut out with a jackknife.)

Capt. Isaac Damon, of Northampton, who belongs to a rather later period, designed and built certainly a half dozen churches, two or three court houses and his fame as a bridge designer and builder in the early part of this century reached far beyond New England.

However, it must be confessed that the larger share of glory belongs to the men classed as amateur architects. Probably they are not amateurs in a strict sense of the word, for many of them received pay for their services; on the other hand, the designing of buildings was an avocation rather than a vocation. To this class of men belongs Joseph Brown, of Providence, born in 1733. He was a merchant and grew rich enough to be independent and then he indulged his natural taste for science. He was particularly interested in electricity and mechanics. He was a member of the American Academy of Arts and Sciences and a trustee of Brown University, and in 1775 he designed the First Baptist Church, still standing in Providence, and his own

house, since destroyed, which 35 years ago was occupied by the Providence Bank. He was sent in 1774 with Mr. Hammond, by the church, to Boston "in order to view the different churches and make a memoranda of their several dimensions and forms of architecture." Another of the Providence amateurs was John Greene, born in Rhode Island in 1777. He designed the First Congregational Meeting House, the Episcopal and the First Universalist churches, and the well-meant restoration in one of these churches along in the middle of the nineteenth century so injured the church in his eyes that he never again attended it.

In Philadelphia, Dr. John Kearsley was the architect of St. Bartholomew's Church, which was built in 1727, and to Andrew Hamilton is ascribed Independence Hall, though authorities differ as to this latter building. Watson's *Annals of Philadelphia* gives Dr. Kearsley the credit for this as well as for Christ Church. Evidently Kearsley and Hamilton were both on the Building Committee for the Hall, and it is probable that Hamilton's plan was used. The latter was educated in London and was a *protégé* of William Penn's and held several high offices in the Province. He died in 1741.

To Thomas Jefferson is ascribed the University of Virginia and several of the more prominent Virginia mansions, including his own house at Monticello, and he collaborated with Clarissault, a French architect, on the Capitol Building at Richmond.

With John McComb, born in 1763, who died in 1853, and whose work includes the city hall in New York and St. John's Church, built at the beginning of this century, begins a period that may be said to deal with

Rear View
FIRST BAPTIST CHURCH—1745—PROVIDENCE,
RHODE ISLAND

Interior
FIRST BAPTIST CHURCH, PROVIDENCE, RHODE ISLAND

the modern architects—Bulfinch, L'Enfant, Latrobe. The works and lives of these men are well known and they are hardly more than a generation removed from our own.

What training or education the American architects of the eighteenth century may have had, I do not know, as I have been unable to find any clear evidences that any of them worked with, or were apprenticed to, English architects.

In many cases this has seemed probable and several of the more prominent men mentioned are said to have been assistants to some of the better known English architects.

As I have said above, it seems to me much more probable that most of the inspiration came through the published works which were to a considerable extent imported from England, and I have appended a short list* of some of these works. There are, doubtless, a good many others of which I do not know, and I do know that the books in the list are to be found quite generally in New England, sometimes in public libraries and sometimes in private families where they have been kept for a hundred years, or since their publication.

There are in the list a very few books published in this country and it would be interesting if some one better fitted than myself could make a much fuller catalogue of these earliest American works on architecture.

A FEW IDENTIFIED BUILDINGS

The dates merely approximate the time of the designer's activity.

ALLYS, JOHN [1665–1700].
  Churches in West Springfield, Hatfield and Hadley, Massachusetts.
AMES, JOHN [1814].
  Churches at Ashfield and Northboro [?], Massachusetts.
BENJAMIN, ASHER [1790].
  Carew House, Springfield; Hollister House, Greenfield; Alexander House, Springfield; West Church, Boston; Colton House, Agawam. All in Massachusetts.
BANNER, PETER [1810].
  Park Street Church, Boston, Massachusetts.
BROWN, JOSEPH [1775].
  First Baptist Church; Providence Bank, Providence, Rhode Island.
BULFINCH, CHARLES.
  State House, Boston, Massachusetts, 1795; State House, Augusta, Maine, 1832; Court house, Worcester, Massachusetts, 1801; Court house, Cambridge, Massachusetts, 1805; State Prison, Charlestown, Massachusetts, 1804; Massachusetts General Hospital, Boston, Massachusetts, 1818; University Hall, Cambridge, Massachusetts, 1814;

New North Church, Boston, 1804; Meeting houses at Pittsfield, Weymouth, Taunton and Lancaster, Massachusetts, and Peterboro, New Hampshire, and many other buildings not now standing.

DAMON, ISAAC [1804].

First Church in Northampton; First Church in Springfield; Church in Pittsfield; Court house in Pittsfield; Court house in Lenox; North Church in Ware. All in Massachusetts. Bridges across the Connecticut at Charlestown, New Hampshire, Springfield and Chicopee; and across the Penobscot, Hudson and Ohio rivers.

ELDERKIN, JOHN [1660].

First Church and Parsonage, New London, Connecticut.

GREENE, JOHN [1814 (?)].

First Congregational, Episcopal and First Universalist Churches, Providence, Rhode Island.

HAMILTON, ANDREW [1735].

Independence Hall, Philadelphia, Pennsylvania.

HOOKER, PHILIP [1813].

Boys' Academy, Albany, New York.

HARRISON, PETER [1760].

Christ Church, Cambridge, Massachusetts; Town Market, Redwood Library and Jewish Synagogue, Newport, Rhode Island.

HOADLEY, DAVID [1812].

North Church, New Haven, Connecticut.

JEFFERSON, THOMAS.

University of Virginia and Monticello, Charlottesville, Virginia.

JOHNSON, EBENEZER [1815].

United Church, New Haven, Connecticut.

KEARSLEY, DR. JOHN [1727].

St. Bartholomew's and Christ Church, Philadelphia, Pennsylvania.

MUNDAY, RICHARD [1783].

Town hall, Newport, Rhode Island.

MCBEAN, ———— [1764].

St. Paul's Chapel, New York.

MCCOMB, JOHN [1803–15].

St. John's Chapel and City Hall, New York, New York.

MCINTIRE, SAMUEL [1806].

South Church, Salem, Massachusetts.

PELL, EDWARD [1721].

North Church, Hanover Street, Boston, Massachusetts.

RHODES, SAMUEL [1770 (?)].

Pennsylvania Hospital, Philadelphia, Pennsylvania.

SMIBERT, JOHN [1742].

Fanueil Hall, Boston, Massachusetts.

SMITH, ROBERT.

Carpenters' Hall, Philadelphia, Pennsylvania.

SPRATZ, WM. [1776–78].

Deming House, Litchfield, Connecticut, and Cowles House, Farmington, Connecticut.

TWELVES, ROBERT [1730].

South Church, Boston, Massachusetts.

WOODRUFF, JUDAH [1769–90].

Gay House, Congregational Church, Samuel Cowles House, Major Hooker House, Wm. Whitman House, Romanta Norton House. All in Farmington, Connecticut.

*BOOKS USED BY THE EARLY ARCHITECTS

ADAMS, R. & S. *Works in Architecture.* 1773–1822.

BENJAMIN, A., AND RAYNERD, D. *The American Builder's Companion.* 44 Plates. Boston, 1806.

BENJAMIN, ASHER. *The Rudiments of Architecture.* Boston, First Edition, 1814; Second Edition, 1820. *Hand-book of Architecture.* Boston, 1834. *Country Builder's Assistant.* Greenfield, 1796.

CAMPBELL, C. *Vitruvius Britannicus.* London, 1715–1725. *The Builder's Dictionary, or Gentleman's and Architect's Companion.* 2 Volumes, 33 Plates. London, 1734.

GIBBS, J. *Rules for drawing the Several Parts of Architecture.* London, 1753.

JONES, I. *Designs consisting of Plans and Elevations for Public and Private Buildings.* Published by W. Kent, London, 1770.

JONES, I., AND OTHERS. *Designs published by Ware, I.* London, 1756.

LANGLEY, B. *The City and Country Builder's and Workman's Treasury of Designs.* 200 Plates. London, 1756.

LANGLEY, B. & T. *Builder's Jewel.* London, 1763.

LANGLEY, T. *Builder's Jewel.* No date.

NORMAN, J. *The Town and Country Builder's Assistant.* 59 Plates. Boston, 1786.

PAIN, WILLIAM. *The Practical Builder, or Workman's General Assistant.* The Fourth Edition, 83 Plates. Boston, 1792.

SOANE, SIR J. *Sketches in Architecture.* 52 Plates. London, 1793.

SWAN, A. *The British Architect or Builder's Treasury of Staircases, etc.* 60 Plates. London, 1745.

Stairs in the Rotunda
CITY HALL, NEW YORK, NEW YORK
John McComb, Architect

CITY HALL, NEW YORK, NEW YORK
John McComb, Architect

View in the Rotunda
CITY HALL, NEW YORK, NEW YORK
John McComb, Architect

CITY HALL, NEW YORK, NEW YORK
John McComb, Architect

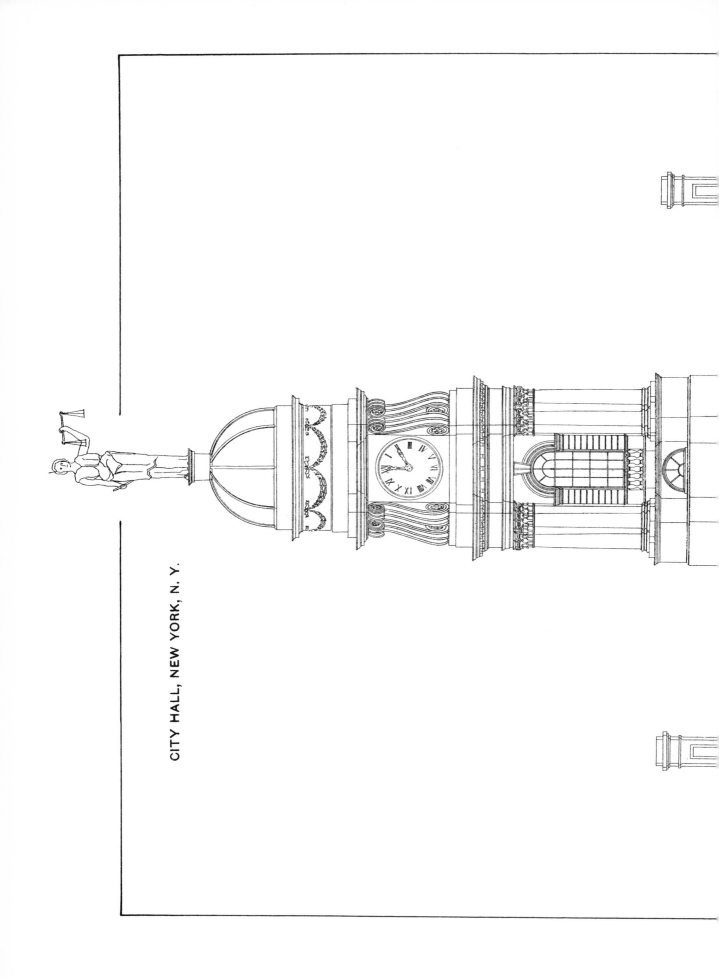

CITY HALL, NEW YORK, N. Y.

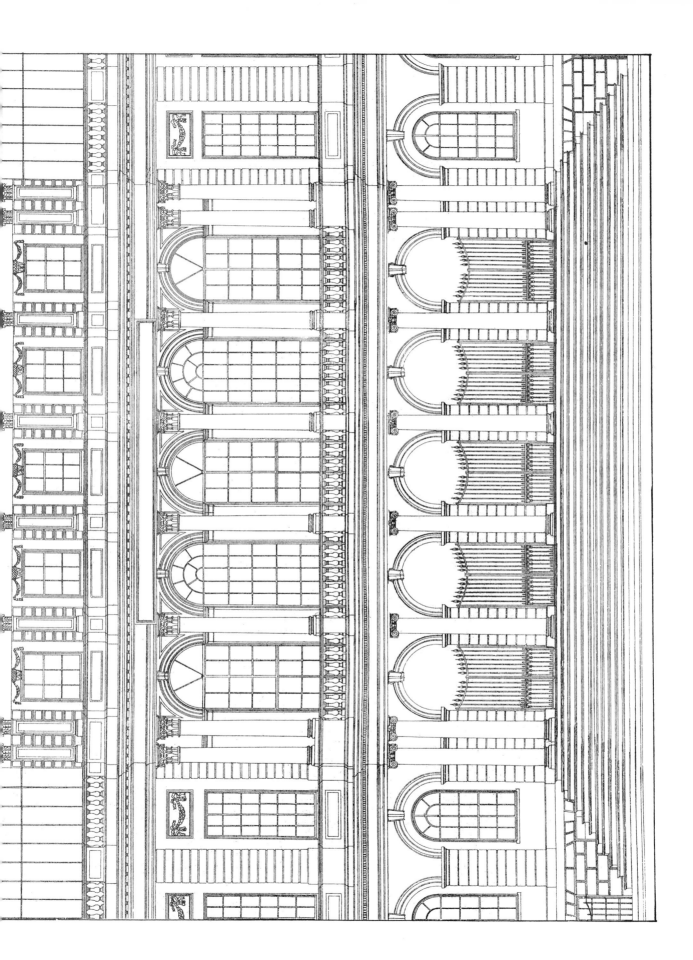

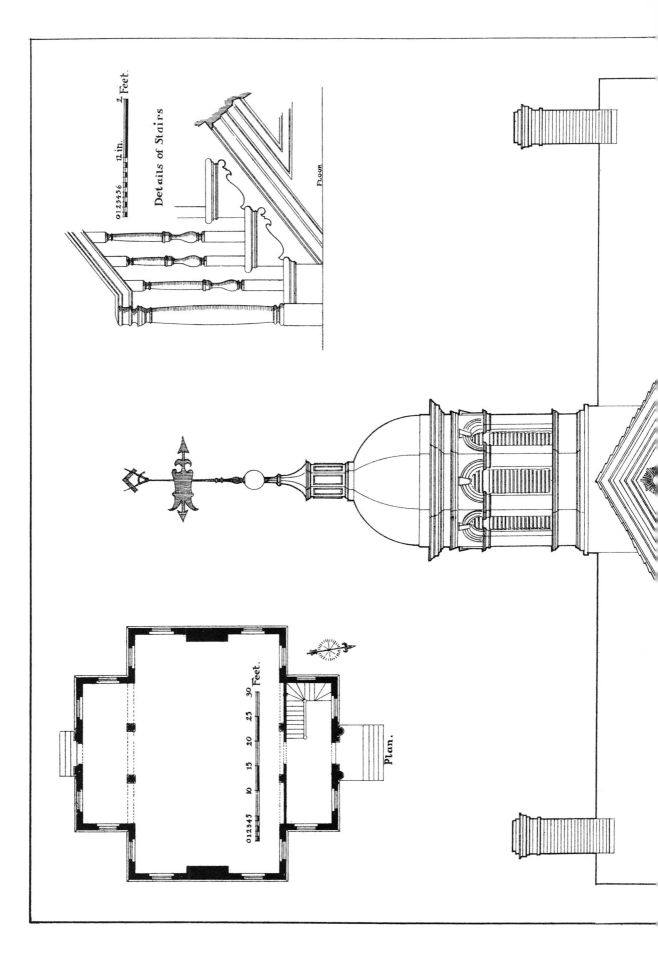

Details of Stairs

0 1 2 3 4 5 6   12 in.   2 Feet.

FLOOR

Plan.

0 1 2 3 4 5   10   15   20   25   30   Feet.

0 1 2 3 4 5   10   15   20 Feet.   North · Front.

CARPENTERS' HALL, *Philadelphia, Pa.*

Measured and drawn by Chas. L. Hillman.

Built 1770 – 1775.
Robert Smith, Archt.
The First Continental Congress
met in this building, 1774.

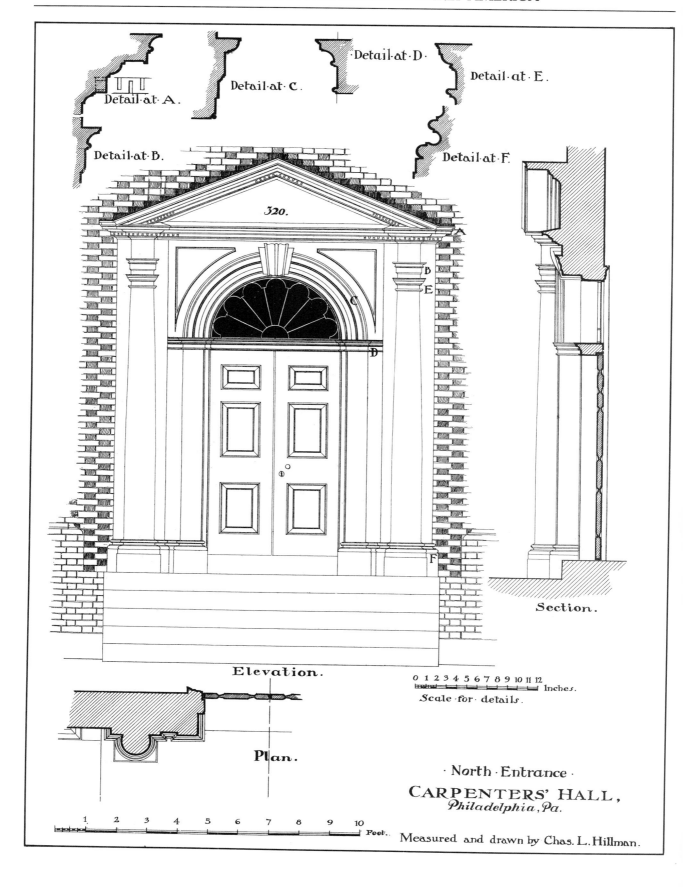

Detail·at·A.

Detail·at·C.

·Detail·at·D·

Detail·at·E.

Detail·at·B.

Detail·at·F.

320.

Section.

Elevation.

0 1 2 3 4 5 6 7 8 9 10 11 12 Inches.
Scale·for·details.

Plan.

1   2   3   4   5   6   7   8   9   10   Feet.

·North·Entrance·

CARPENTERS' HALL,
Philadelphia, Pa.

Measured and drawn by Chas. L. Hillman.

THE OLD WEST CHURCH, CAMBRIDGE STREET, BOSTON, MASS.
REMODELLED INTERNALLY IN 1895, AND NOW USED AS A BRANCH OF THE BOSTON PUBLIC LIBRARY.
MEASURED AND DRAWN BY MR. A. C. FERNALD. PROBABLE ARCHITECT, ASHER BENJAMIN.

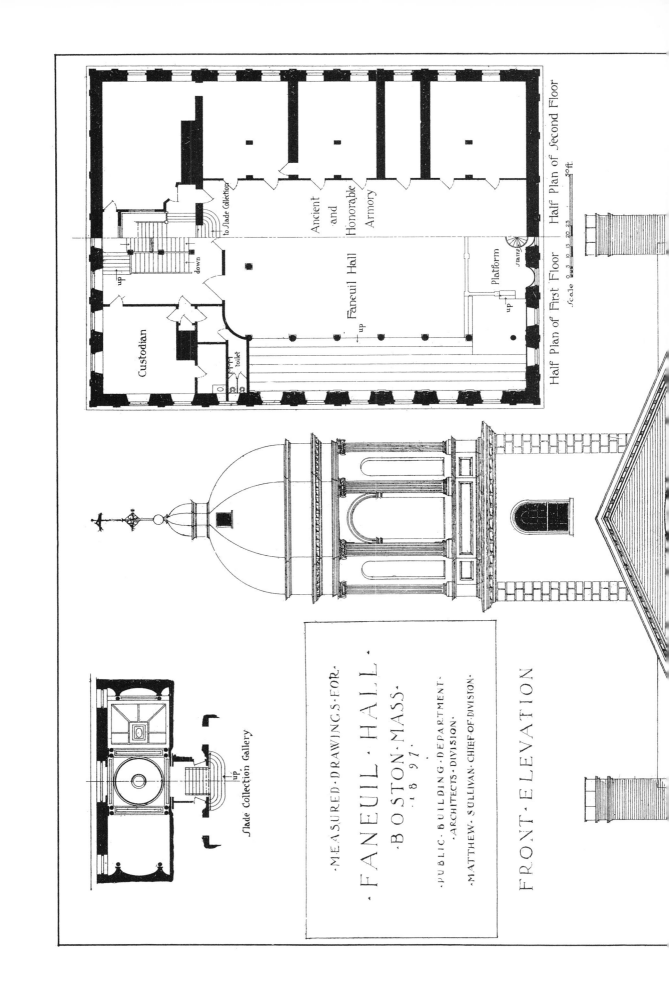

Half Plan of First Floor   Half Plan of Second Floor

Scale 0 5 10 15 20 25   30 ft.

to Slade Collection

Ancient
and
Honorable
Armory

Faneuil Hall

Platform

stairs

up

up

down

up

Custodian

toilet

Slade Collection Gallery

up

· MEASURED · DRAWINGS · FOR ·

· FANEUIL · HALL ·

· BOSTON · MASS ·

· 1 8 9 7 ·

· PUBLIC · BUILDING · DEPARTMENT ·

· ARCHITECTS · DIVISION ·

· MATTHEW · SULLIVAN · CHIEF · OF · DIVISION ·

FRONT · ELEVATION

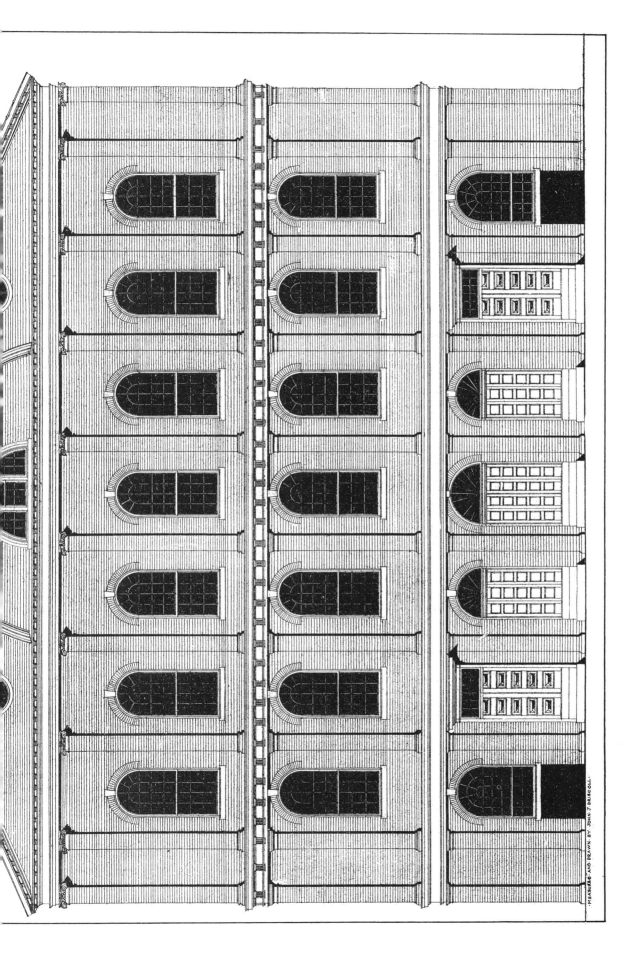

·MEASURED· AND· DRAWN· BY· JOHN· J· DRISCOLL·

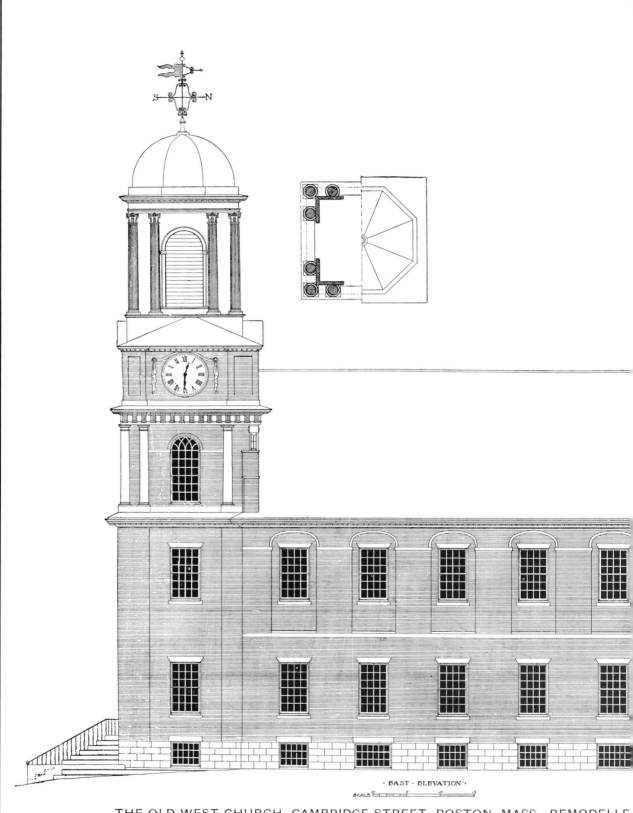

· EAST · ELEVATION ·

SCALE

THE OLD WEST CHURCH, CAMBRIDGE STREET, BOSTON, MASS., REMODELLE

MEASURED AND DRAWN BY MR. A. C. FERNALD

W E

FRONT ELEVATION

SCALE

TERNALLY IN 1895 AND NOW USED AS A BRANCH OF THE BOSTON PUBLIC LIBRARY.
OBABLE ARCHITECT, ASHER BENJAMIN.

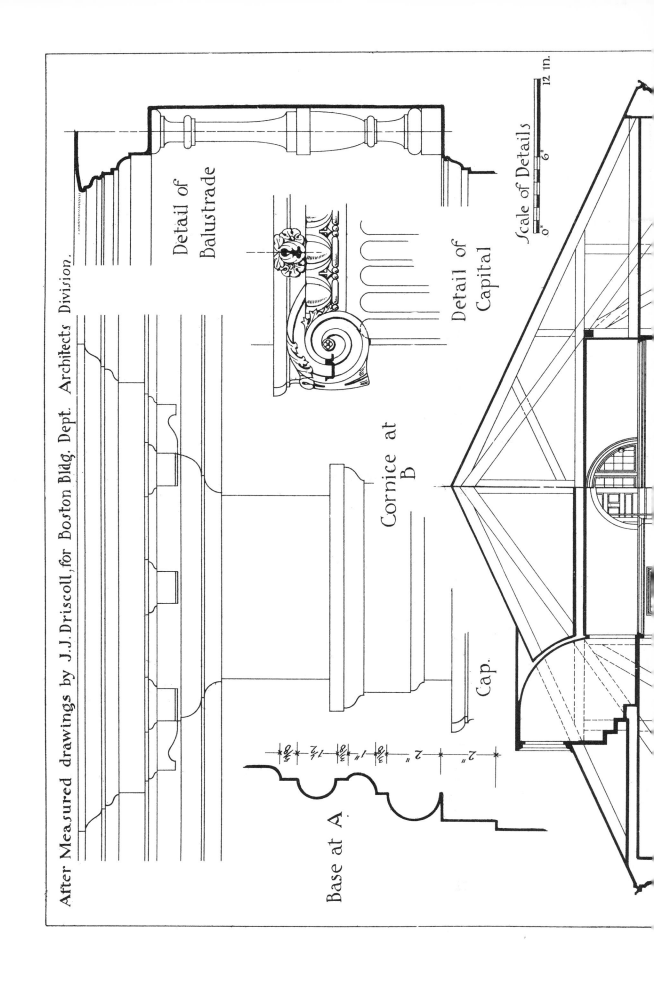

After Measured drawings by J.J. Driscoll, for Boston Bldg. Dept. Architects Division.

Detail of Balustrade

Detail of Capital

Cornice at B

Cap.

Base at A.

Scale of Details

0"   6'   12 in.

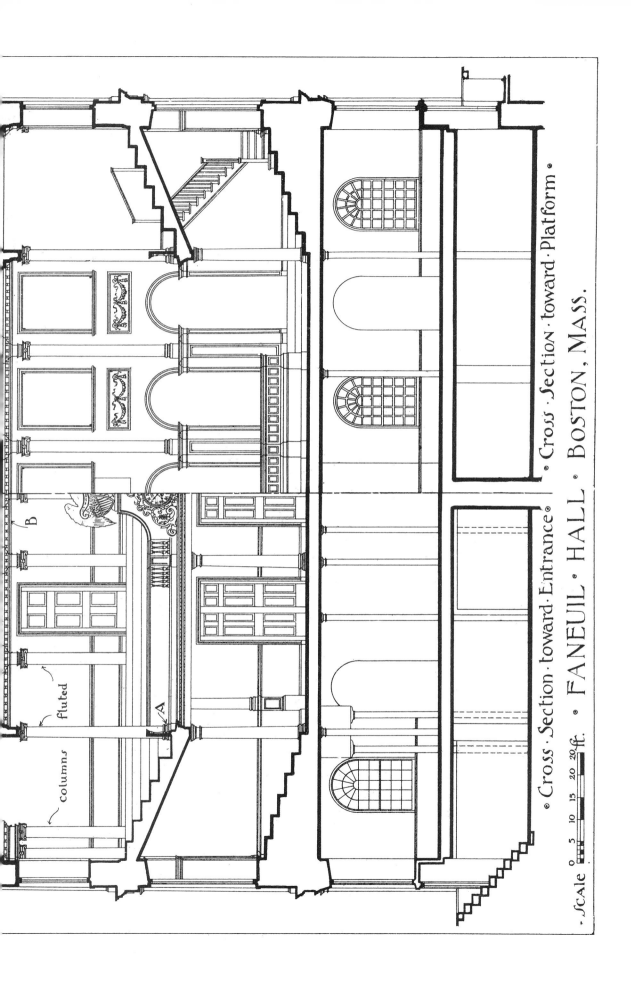

columns

fluted

B

A

° Cross · Section · toward · Entrance °

° Cross · Section · toward · Platform °

FANEUIL · HALL · BOSTON, MASS.

· Scale · 0 5 10 15 20 20 ft.

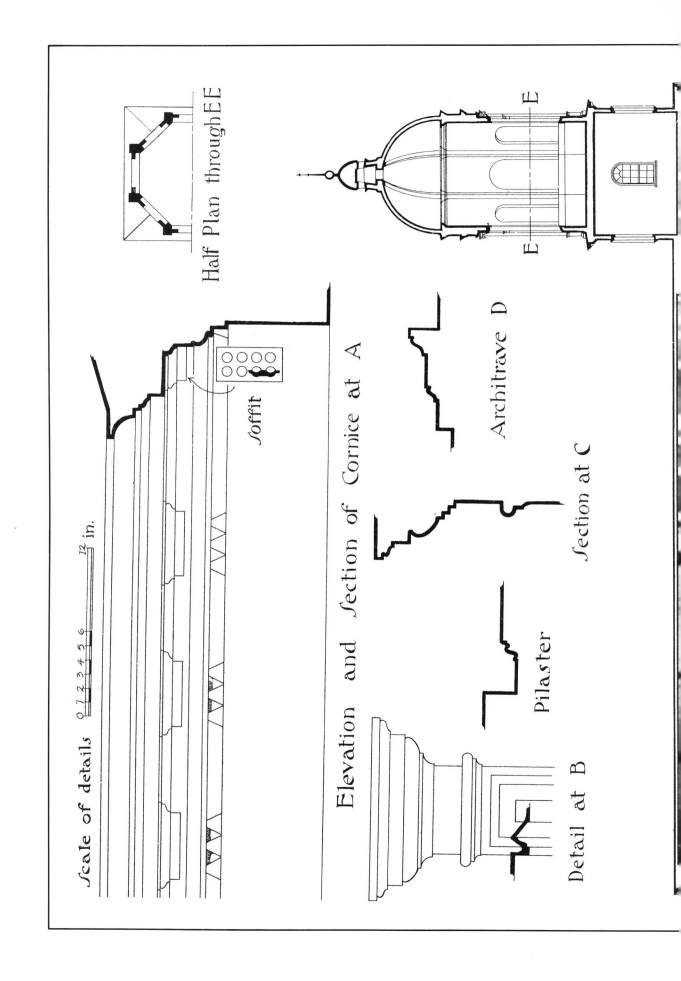

Half Plan through EE

E

E

Scale of details

0 1 2 3 4 5 6   12 in.

Soffit

Elevation and Section of Cornice at A

Architrave D

Section at C

Pilaster

Detail at B

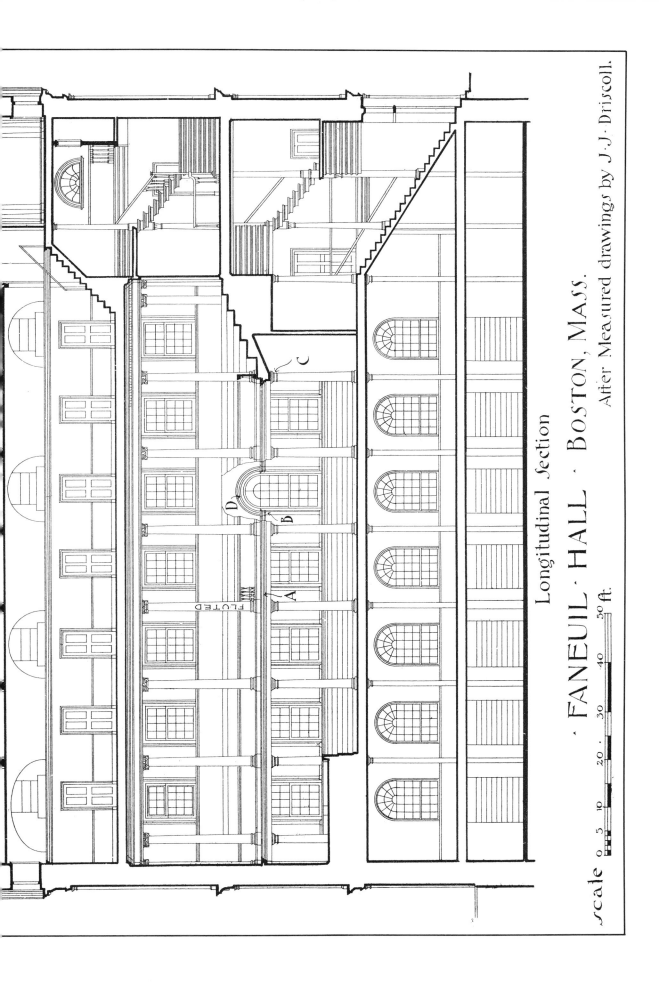

FLUTED

A
B
C
D

Longitudinal Section

· FANEUIL · HALL · BOSTON, MASS.

After Measured drawings by J·J· Driscoll.

Scale 0 5 10 20 30 40 50 ft.

· Front Entrance of the Jas · L · Cowles House ·
· Farmington · Conn ·

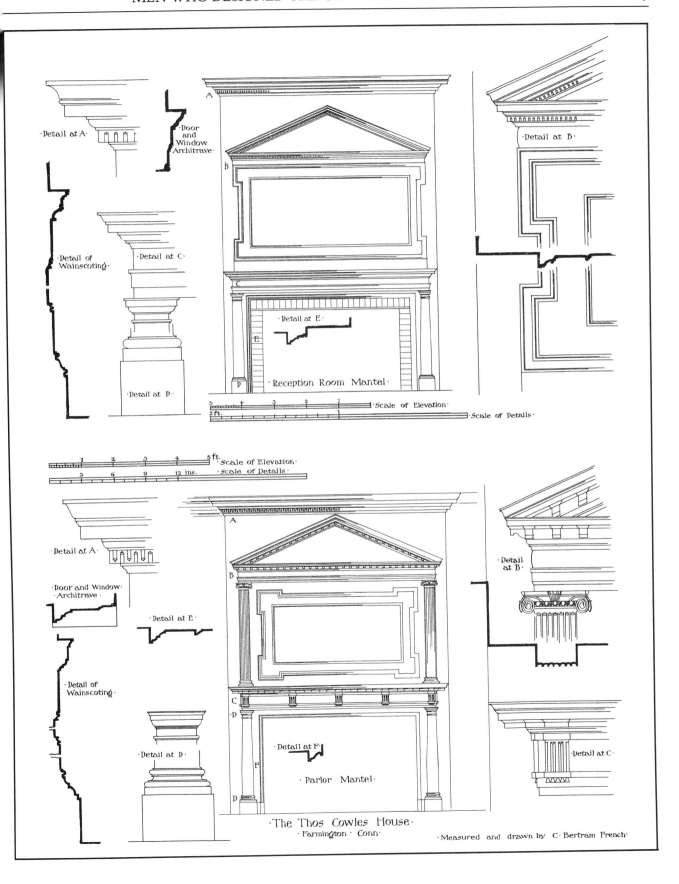

·Detail at A·

·Door
and
Window
Architrave·

·Detail of
Wainscoting·

·Detail at C·

·Detail at D·

·Detail at B·

A

B

C

·Detail at E·

E

D

·Reception Room Mantel·

5 4   3   2   1   ·Scale of Elevation·
2 ft.   ·Scale of Details·

1   2   3   4   5 ft. ·Scale of Elevation·
3   6   9   12 ins. ·Scale of Details·

·Detail at A·

·Door and Window·
·Architrave·

·Detail at E·

·Detail of
Wainscoting·

·Detail at D·

·Detail
at B·

A

B

·Detail at F·

C
·D

F

D

·Parlor Mantel·

·Detail at C·

·The Thos Cowles House·
·Farmington · Conn·

·Measured and drawn by C· Bertram French·

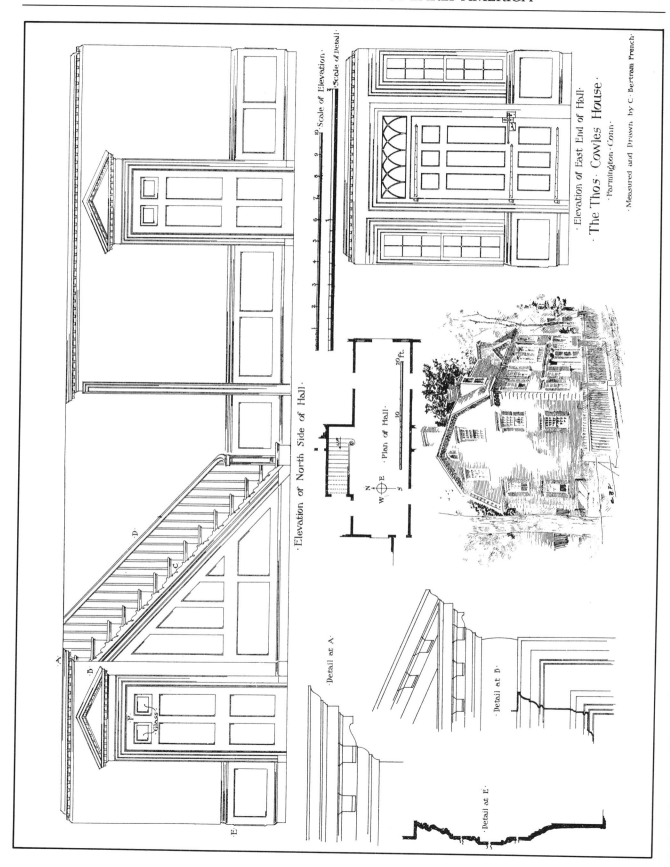

·Scale of Elevation·

·Scale of Detail·

·Elevation of East End of Hall·

·The Thos· Cowles· House·

·Farmington· Conn·

·Measured and Drawn by C· Bertram French·

·Elevation of North Side of Hall·

·Plan of Hall·

·Glass·

·Detail at A·

·Detail at B·

·Detail at E·

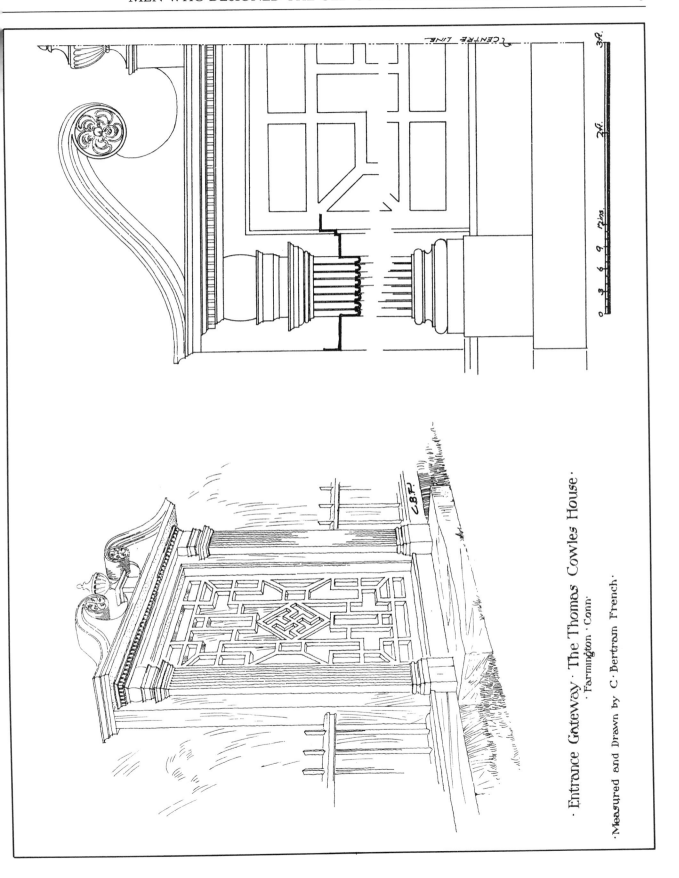

· Entrance Gateway · The Thomas Cowles House ·
· Farmington · Conn ·

· Measured and Drawn by C · Bertram French ·

South Door
STATE HOUSE, PHILADELPHIA, PENNSYLVANIA

Hotel Cluny of
a New England Village

Text by
Sylvester Baxter
Originally published in 1900 as
Volume II of The Georgian Period

WHIPPLE HOUSE, IPSWICH, MASSACHUSETTS

THE HOTEL CLUNY OF A NEW ENGLAND VILLAGE

THE extraordinary production and huge circulation of the historical novel is but one of the consequences of the remarkable growth of the "patriotic societies" in this country in the past few years — societies like those of the Sons and the Daughters of the Revolution, the Colonial Dames, and the like. One of the most admirable results of the movement is the widespread interest in the establishment of local historical societies, particularly in the old towns of New England. These historical societies have a very interesting and even fascinating work before them: the collection and preservation of all manner of local records, the looking up of spots of historical interest, the preservation of interesting old buildings, and the marking of historic sites with commemorative tablets, besides the study and discussion of both local and general history. In the average New England town the soil proves gratifyingly fertile in these fields and the delving therein bears rich fruit in the development of interest in and love for the community, the heightening of civic feeling, the encouragement of local improvements, and a care for the future of the town as well as an interest in the town's past.

In not a few places the local historical society has done a most excellent thing by taking some fine or quaint old house for its headquarters, fitting it up after old fashions, and adorning it with attractive historical collections. Such a collection on a large scale is that of the Bostonian Society, to which the city long ago gave the free use of the picturesque Old State House, above the ground floor, and has converted the old-time halls of legislation in the carefully restored building into a rich museum of all manner of antiquities relating to the history of Boston. Medford is a fine colonial town with a goodly number of stately old dwellings. One of these, the Cradock House, built in the year 1632 for Governor Cradock of the Massachusetts Bay Colony — who never came over from England to occupy it — is reputed to be the oldest dwelling in the original portion of the United States. Singularly enough, this has very lately been established to be not the picturesque brick house that has long gone by that name and which is a very close reproduction of a typical English farmhouse, but is identical with what is known as the Garrison House,[1] in the center of the city, still occupied as a very comfortable and prosperous looking dwelling. The highly active Medford His-

torical Society — a member of which unearthed in London the map and other documents that attested this important fact — had once endeavored to secure for its headquarters the fine old Royall House with its extensive grounds, a particularly imposing mansion of pre-Revolutionary days, but the owners would not part with it. Its use, however, was secured as the scene of a notable historical festival given by the Society a few years ago. The Society thereupon contented itself with more modest quarters, but most attractively and appropriately fitted up, in the shape of the old-fashioned house that has an historical interest in American literature, and in the antislavery movement, as the birthplace of Lydia Maria Child.

In certain respects, however, the most notable accomplishment in this direction is the work of the Ipswich Historical Society in the restoration of an ancient dwelling to its primitive condition as it existed in the primal days of the Massachusetts Bay Colony. This work has been done with such fidelity, such fine appreciation and understanding, and the house, with its collections, is intrinsically so full of interest, that it deserves wide celebrity, both as an example of what might be accomplished in not a few other places, and as one of the most interesting sights for visitors to New England.

For the latter, the quaint old town of Ipswich is in itself well worth going far to see. Although one of the most traveled lines of railway on the continent passes through it, the beautiful old town has preserved its ancient charms in a sort of isolation amidst the wide levels of the vast salt marshes that spread before it. The clear Ipswich River rambles gently down from the inland hills, and here, in the heart of the town, tumbles in falls down to the tidal level, thence meander-

---

[1] Although we have no illustration of the Garrison House at Medford, the title recalls the fact that a structure locally known by the same name at Newburyport, Massachusetts, and like the Medford building presumably deriving its name from the fact of its one-time use as stronghold or block-house for the little settlement was described in Chapter 1 of Volume XIII and we take the opportunity to introduce on page 221 an illustration of the building as it now exists. To balance the effect of the picture of the Garrison House, at Newburyport, we introduce on page 222 an illustration of another old house in the same quaint seaport. It is a typical of many dwellings throughout New England and wherever these are seen, even when standing in absolute isolation in the midst of a barren shore-pasture they attract attention and admiration because of their air of thorough homelikeness, and in more than one of them interesting interior features are to be found. — WARE

ing through the marshes to the sea, whence vessels come and go at the wharves that were once the scenes of a lively commerce in the days when all the coast ports were havens for maritime adventurings. Skirting the river are the quiet winding streets, shaded by great elms and bordered by many fine old houses. Just over the town there rises the noble drumlin shape of Heartbreak Hill like a gigantic billow—celebrated in a poem by the late Lucy Larcom that tenderly records the legend of the Indian maiden who, from its summit, daily looked in vain for the coming of her lover. It is true that upon a last-century map of the town the designation of "Hard Brick Hill" is inscribed. But good authority declares this to be a prosaic and ignorant corruption of the original name.

The charms of the town itself and the loveliness of the environing landscape make Ipswich a favorite resort for artists through the summer. The scenery is that which Mr. J. Appleton Brown loves to paint, pastoral and idyllic, with its rolling uplands, its tranquil waters and its placid marshes that enter in among the hills in mysterious tree-fringed bays and coves. Artists come hither by the score to feast upon the beauty of the countryside. And Ipswich is the home of two painters of national repute, Mr. Arthur W. Dow, whose birthplace it is and who has found here many of his strikingly original themes; and Mr. Theodore Wendel, whose wife is a daughter of the town.

It would be difficult to arrange a more delightful excursion for a summer day than to start out early in the morning from Boston on a trolley trip to Ipswich by way of Lynn and Salem and through the diversified scenery of Essex County, arriving in time to inspect the old Whipple House, and then, after luncheon, taking the little steamboat that plies between Ipswich and Newburyport twice a day upon a fascinating voyage down the river and by the inside route through Plum Island Sound, whose quiet waters, shallow and variegated with delicate shadings of green and blue, are sheltered from the tossing Atlantic by the long and narrow insular barrier of sand dunes. From Newburyport a train will bring one back to Boston in an hour or so. Or, one may extend the day's pleasuring by taking another steamboat up the Marrimac, Whittier's beautiful river, and there find a train for Boston.

The Hôtel Cluny, as all know, is a magnificent old French château preserved exactly as in the ancient days, and filled with a priceless collection of objects representative of the life of its day. It sets an example of what may wisely be done with fine old buildings elsewhere—though the example may more wisely be bettered by a better arrangement and classification of the collections shown therein than has been effected at the Hôtel Cluny. It is a far cry, of course, from the superb Parisian château, and the splendors for which it stands, to the austere Puritan age and land when our mighty country was all one frontier, facing the ocean on one side and the savage wilderness on the other, with a meager fringe of settlements. But the Whipple House, of Ipswich, like the Hôtel Cluny, of Paris, represents the best of its day, and it stands as, probably, the most faithful reproduction yet achieved of the home environment of the primitive colonial life of New England in the days when our ancestors, with their stern beliefs, their harsh moralities, their appalling superstitions, might be regarded as little more than barbarians, when measured by the standards of today.

The visitor to Ipswich by train finds the Whipple House just across the way from the station, towards which its low-walled back is turned in accordance with the ancient rule that faced all houses to the south when standing detached. Venerably homely, in the truest sense of the word, and restored to its original aspect as carefully as the most scholarly research and the most scrupulous adherence to ascertained facts can make it possible, it is certainly one of the most notable old houses in the United States. The simple beauty of its setting is in striking harmony with its character. This environment, indeed, is doubtless less austere than that of the house in its primitive days. But in its quaint charm it reproduces the effect of the grounds of the Colonial mansion at their best, a century later; grounds such as this house may then well have possessed. And a work of this character and public importance, truly monumental in intention, demands surroundings that betoken the esteem in which it is held.

When the work was undertaken it seemed an heroic task to effect creditable results from the conditions into which the house and its vicinage had fallen from their once high estate. The structure was shabby and dilapidated with misuse, and mutilated by various successive reconstructions, while its surroundings were of the depressingly squalid character that so frequently obtains in the neighborhood of a railway, even in a good old rural town. But intelligence and energy soon radically changed the face of things. The head and front of the Ipswich Historical Society is its president, the Rev. T. Frank Waters, pastor of the Trinitarian Congregational Church, and throwing himself into the work with heart and soul, the ancient house seemed to resume its proper guise as if under the touch of magic. As the investigations necessary to the required repairs proceeded, the original state and shape of the building were gradually revealed sufficiently to afford a sure guidance in the work of restoration. This work, however, could not possibly have been so complete, had not the mechanics employed

GARRISON HOUSE, NEWBURYPORT,
MASSACHUSETTS

given themselves to the work with an enthusiastic devotion. And the existence among these of names like Sullivan and Thibedeau, besides names savoring of the soil, like Choate, Goditt and Lord, show how completely the late-coming elements assimilate themselves to the New England spirit of the best old communities. Mr. Thibedeau, for instance, though employed as a carpenter, was specially commended by the committee in charge for his wonderful patience and persistence in giving weeks of hard and painstaking toil to scraping and scrubbing the woodwork, always standing in perfect readiness to do anything however far removed from his natural province. It is particularly gratifying to note these facts, testifying to the persistence of the old spirit of the artisan who finds pleasure in his work, when so much is said nowadays about the decline of the modern mechanic and his departure from old-time standards. But in this instance, with the good old New England "faculty" guiding the work, from the highest to the lowest, and practically the whole community showing the deepest interest, the ends were achieved with astonishing economy and completeness. The sum of $1,650 purchased the place, and an expenditure of only a little more than a thousand dollars accomplished this commendable work of

restoration and created one of the finest historical monuments in the country, a perfect specimen of the seventeenth-century architecture of New England.

In the course of restoration all the decayed spots were cut out of the ancient beams and new wood was skillfully inserted, the exterior was newly clapboarded and shingled — clapboards, it seems, preceded shingles as a covering for outside walls; diamond-paned windows, low and broad, replaced the perpendicular and narrow ones that an ugly later fashion had given the house, and a coat of dark stain restored the exterior fully to its old-time aspect.

Within, comparatively modern changes had much subdivided the four great rooms into which the main part of the house was originally divided. All the partitions were removed and the rooms were restored to their old shape. In each was built a huge fireplace in the old style. When the plaster ceilings were torn away the original floor-joists of hewn oak were revealed, with the original plastering between them. The big beams and the joists were carefully scraped and oiled, and the contrast between their rich brown hue and the white of the plaster between them gave to the large rooms with their very low ceilings — which a person of average height can easily touch with his hand — an ap-

COLLINS HOUSE, NEWBURYPORT,
MASSACHUSETTS

pearance that is picturesque, and at the same time is dignified with the air of old-time stateliness. As the president said in his report at the first annual meeting of the Society, celebrating the achievement of one of its prime declared objects in "the preservation of and finishing in Colonial style of one of the ancient dwelling-houses of said Ipswich": "The size and quality of these superb oak-beams, their finely finished moulded edges, the substantial oak floor joists, the great posts, with their escutcheons so laboriously wrought, the noble size of these four great rooms, proclaim that this was a home of wealth and refinement, and make it easy for us to believe that it was the finest mansion of the town."

The work of restoration required patience, thoroughness and delicacy. All the woodwork had to be laboriously and carefully scoured to remove the grime and whitewash with which it was coated in layer after layer. The process of reconstruction was fascinating to follow in its revelation of the peculiarities of ancient methods of house-building. The spaces between the studs, from sill to plate, were found filled in with brickwork, and this was preserved so far as possible. In one of the chambers, the manner of this construction is exhibited by means of a plate of glass set into the

wall and framed with the care that might be shown for a treasured old master. The places where the handsome old windows were was shown with exactness, and their restoration proved one of the most effective features of the house, bringing it closer into relation with its models across the sea, where the same form of window is today in common use. It was of course easy to disclose the fireplaces that had been shut in to allow the substitution of the ugly and economical stove. But these were small fireplaces of comparatively modern date, nesting within the enormous originals built of stone—the latter so well preserved that it was an easy matter to restore them in all their completeness. Much of the old plastering was so perfect that it did not have to be touched. And, by way of experiment, for a deal of the new work made necessary to replace the old plastering, the ancient fashion of making a compound of clay, sand and salt hay was tried with entire success.

Exactly how old the house is has not yet been ascertained. But it certainly dates back to the middle of the seventeenth century, and possibly a house that stood on the place when its sale to Mr. John Whipple, an eminent man of Ipswich, was completed by a quit-claim deed from John Fawne in the year 1650, may have formed a portion of it. Mr. John Whipple had been living on the spot since 1642 at least. It has been well established, however, that in the first years of the colony the Puritans very seldom built the roomy and comfortable dwellings that it has been supposed they did. Their first abodes were huts and dugouts, inferior to the rude dwellings of the pioneers on the prairies of the West. Some years passed before the accepted Colonial home, even in its humblest shape, began to appear with the development of well-being in the land. Even the rough shanty where Italian laborers huddle would have been deemed luxurious by our Puritan ancestors in their first years in the New World.

The Whipple House in its present shape is a growth formed by successive enlargements made in the course of a considerable number of years. In its original shape it apparently consisted of what is now the western half of the main portion. First the house was doubled in size and then two successive additions were made in the rear, giving it the long sloping roof on the north side so characteristic of many old farmhouses. In its present shape, therefore, the house in its very old portion comprises four remarkably large rooms, two on the ground-floor and two above, each with a fireplace big enough to contain great logs of wood. In the adaptation of the house to the uses of the Historical Society, and its conversion into what may be called a museum of the ancient New England home, each of these four rooms, with its collections, has been given a typical character.

First and chief of these comes the "hall" in the great east room. This is by no means the hall of the eighteenth-century Colonial mansion—the spacious entrance room, with its stately staircase, running through the center of the house. Here the front door is likewise in the middle, but a tall man must stoop to enter, and keep stooping while in the diminutive entry, where a steep and narrow flight of stairs twists itself upward besides the gigantic chimney-stack that shows how its original size was doubled when the house was. In New England, as in old, the hall was the common gathering-place of the family—the place where the meals were cooked and eaten, where the spinning and weaving was done, where the household came together to enjoy the heat and the light of the enormous fire on the hearth beneath a chimney which, as Mr. Waters tells us, was ample enough to allow boys on mischief bent to drop a live calf from the roof, as they did one night into poor old Mark Quilter's kitchen. It was often a scene of much jollity, we may believe, for the Puritans could not always and universally have maintained their traditional austerity. And the room was so spacious that we may be sure that it invited to no little frolicsomeness among the young folks, and we may even fancy that at times the floor was cleared for a

bouncing good dance. So the place was a "hall" in the amplest sense of the word. It was not until a much later date that the room became exclusively a kitchen. And our Irish fellow-citizen, even though he may have rolled up wealth in city contracts, is but perpetuating the traditions of the baronial hall when he insists on spending his home hours sitting by the kitchen stove in his shirt-sleeves, with clay pipe in mouth.

The beautiful old hall of the Whipple House is a fascinating gallery of the quaint utensils of domestic and industrial use in the old-time New England home—everything that entered into kitchen-service, barn-service, field-service, spinning, weaving, etc., beside various things whose purposes the most patient research, the most ingenious conjecture, have not yet been able to discover. We laugh at the clumsiness of certain of these utensils, but we are compelled to admire the simple way in which many others met the needs of the time. Clever examples of Yankee, or pre-Yankee, ingenuity are some of these things: for instance, the "cradlechurn," where the milk was contained in a long, trough-like receptacle mounted lengthwise on rockers. As the housewife and others went about their domestic tasks they would give it a touch in passing. This was sufficient to keep it going, and so the butter was made without any appreciable effort.

In the corner of the large west room there remained a fine old buffet as a relic of the olden days. This suggested the wainscoting of the room with some handsome paneling taken from an old house in the town, the Rogers Manse, built in 1728, and given to the Historical Society by the owner. Over the mantel a quaint painted panel representing a panoramic view of Ipswich town from the river, with Heart Break Hill in the background, and the water enlivened with old-fashioned shipping, was inserted. The woodwork was painted white, making a typical eighteenth-century room of it. This is appropriately used for the exhibition of old china and crockery, silver, etc., old-fashioned musical instruments, a collection of rare old books, pamphlets and manuscripts, and many other interesting things.

The east chamber has been made the meeting room of the Society and fitted up after the fashion of an old-style "best room," enriched with many beautiful old curios of historic value. The interest taken in the old house brought to the collections in these three rooms an extraordinary number of antiquities, given or loaned not only by the people of Ipswich, but by friends throughout Essex County and in many other parts of the country.

The west chamber was made the room of the resident caretaker. It was a piece of good fortune for the

WHIPPLE HOUSE, IPSWICH, MASSACHUSETTS

Society to secure for this responsible position a lady of the experience and capacity of Miss Alice A. Gray, curator of the Department of Textiles in the Boston Museum of Fine Arts, and a niece of the famous botanist, the late Prof. Asa Gray. It was equally a pleasure for Miss Gray to make her home in an ideal old-fashioned house and to supervise the arrangement of its fascinating collections. Beside using the west chamber as her office, she has fitted it up as a typical old style "best chamber"—a special addition to the attractions of the house. The rear portion of the house was, moreover, converted into a charming apartment for herself and her housekeeper; a cosy suite with a delightful air of old-fashioned comfort unobtrusively reinforced by the modern conveniences without which life in a house of the kind would be a pastime that a child of the nineteenth century would soon weary of. An attractive feature of this suite is the row of snug little chambers with slant ceilings under the roof on the second floor.

A sort of thorn in the flesh for the Historical Society, after the completion of its task, was the uncomfortable proximity of a most disreputable-looking old tenement house on the rear side, between the ancient mansion and the railway track. But one day Miss Gray had a visit from a Boston friend, a lady whose means enable her to follow her natural inclination to do all sorts of good deeds. The visitor was thoroughly delighted with what had been accomplished, and the next day Miss Gray received from her a check for $2,000 to enable the Society to complete its work by giving its home a suitable environment through getting rid of the adjacent eyesore. With this money not only was the tenement house purchased and demolished, but a new old-fashioned garden was laid out on its site, and about the ancient dwelling: a gay multitude of the blooms cherished by our mothers, our grandmothers, our great grandmothers, and losing no favor in the eyes of ourselves or our children, assemble their gladsome motley before the sober gray of the ancient walls; a box-bordered walk leading up to the caretaker's door past a handsome sundial of stone; a well with its old-time sweep at the side of the house. These touches made the whole complete.

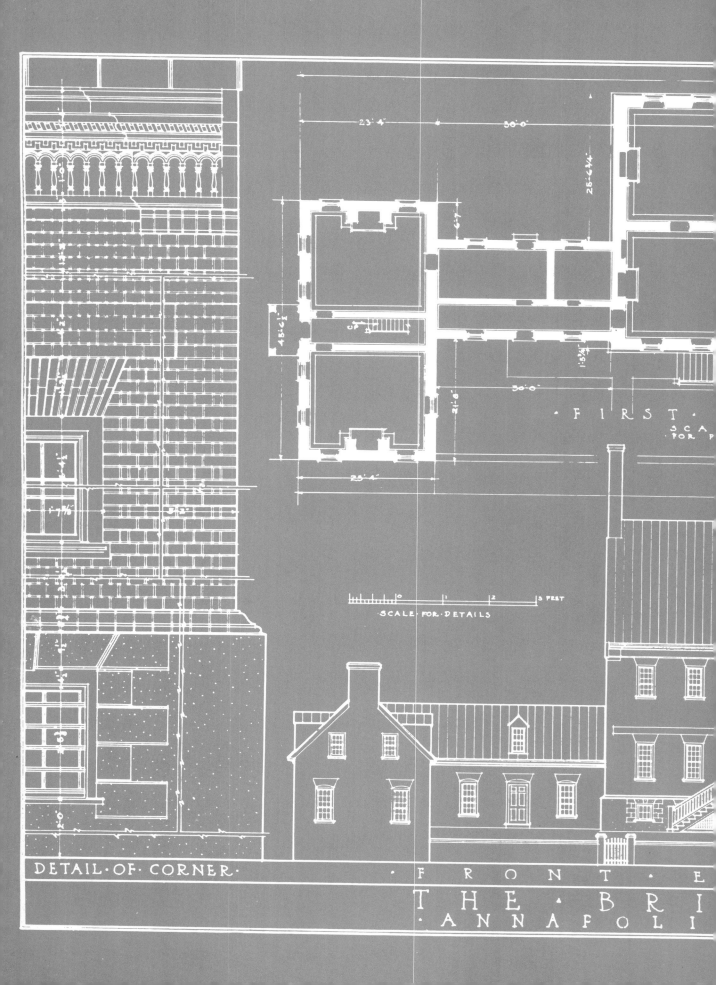

DETAIL·OF·CORNER·

·FIRST·

SCA
·FOR·P

|᠁᠁᠁᠁᠁|0 |1 |2 |3 FEET
·SCALE·FOR·DETAILS·

23'·4"

30'·0"

25'·6¼"

48'·6"

21'·6"

1'·5¼"

30'·0"

23'·4"

·F R O N T · E
T H E · B R I
· A N N A P O L I